Evidence from the Floor

with prophetic insights of Kenny Borthwick

Hugh B. Black
with
Dr Alison H. Black

New Wine Press

New Wine Press
PO Box 17
Chichester PO20 6YB
England

Unless otherwise stated, all biblical references are taken from the Authorised Version.

ISBN: 1 874367 95 7

Other books by Hugh Black
The Baptism in the Spirit and Its Effects
Reflections on the Gifts of the Spirit
Reflections on a Song of Love (1 Corinthians 13)
A Trumpet Call to Women
The Clash of Tongues: With Glimpses of Revival
Consider Him (Twelve Qualities of Christ)
Battle for the Body
The Incomparable Christ
Gospel Vignettes
Reflections from Abraham
Reflections from Moses: With the Testimony of Daniel McVicar
Christ the Deliverer
Christian Fundamentals
Reflections from David
Pioneers of the Spiritual Way
Revival: Including the Prophetic Vision of Jean Darnall
Revival: Personal Encounters
Revival: Living in the Realities
War in Heaven and Earth
E.H. Taylor: A Modern Christian Mystic (edited by Hugh Black)
A View from the Floor
Further Views from the Floor (with Dr A. H. Black)

Typeset by CRB Associates, Reepham, Norfolk
Printed in England by Clays Ltd, St Ives plc.

Dedication

To those who have found the floor of earth
the floor of heaven

Contents

Foreword

As I begin to write I seem to see before me a ship making its way from the confines of a narrow estuary out to the vastness of an ocean, its waters reflecting the rays of a sun just rising on its horizon. The ship has reached the estuary mouth; all on board are viewing, with awe and wonder, what is before them. The full realization waits of what has been seen from afar.

> There to an ocean fullness,
> His mercy doth expand,
> And glory, glory dwelleth
> In Immanuel's land.

This simple picture seems to portray to me what Christ is doing in His church today. He is leading many from the narrowness and restriction of their present experience out into the vastness of His provision. It is, undoubtedly, the beginnings of what so many longing hearts have seen from afar.

We are seeing before our very eyes the mighty acts of the Holy Spirit restoring to the church of Christ all that she had lost, and so much more than the early church knew. Our beloved Lord will return for a church that is not in defeat but in victory – not unclean and under the dominion of sin, but free, without spot or blemish, bearing His likeness.

In this book and in the two previous titles of the trilogy, Mr Black presents the subject of the new ministry with its impact and effects upon many lives, mine being one. The new ministry seemed to coincide with what God was doing in other places. I think of churches such as Holy Trinity, Brompton (London), Vineyard Airport Church (Toronto), followed by the powerful ongoing revival in Brownsville Assemblies of God (Pensacola, Florida). We, like them, have experienced something of this fresh wave of the power of the Holy Spirit which is sweeping over the church of Christ today. I am sure the reader of this book will not fail to be moved and encouraged by the testimonies in it. They are so varied, but all have the touch of divine encounter, each exhibiting some attribute of the Lord Jesus Christ, His power, purity, compassion and love.

I believe that Mr Black ranks as one of the true church's great end-time leaders. His leadership extends far beyond the limits of the Struthers movement. We have a great spiritual legacy encapsulated within the now large selection of his books on vital Christian teaching. Surely, this trumpet has not sounded any uncertain note.

My sincere prayer is that God will quicken and bless richly all who read this book.

Owen E. Martin

Preface

This book is the third in a series that portrays at first-hand the experiences of those who have fallen (often literally) under the power of the Spirit of God. Like its predecessors, *Evidence from the Floor* concentrates on testimonies from within the Struthers movement from November 1994, which saw the dawn of a 'new ministry' under which many went prostrate and encountered Christ deeply. The book also ranges more widely to convey the impact of reports that have come to us from further afield. Of particular interest to all who care about our nation is the story of Kenny Borthwick, minister of the Church of Scotland in Thurso, and the series of his visions presented in the last chapter.

One of the themes to emerge most strikingly is the concern of our God with matters both great and small. In days of increasing political and environmental unrest, He has His finger on the pulse of nations and foresees the outworking of all things to His glory. Yet He is not too remote to catch the smallest whisper from the least of His children. That is why this book ranges from something so seemingly trivial as the healing from a spider phobia to a revival affecting thousands in Mexico. The concept of a God who spans the infinitely small and the infinitely great is, if we stop to think about it, truly breathtaking.

The thought of cataclysmic events, both natural and spiritual, can generate fear. But Christ's word is, 'Fear not, little flock.' Mighty in His moving over the earth, He is present where the tiniest group gathers in His Name. Our God is great beyond imagining – but He is also personal. In the heart of the whirlwind there is peace. To Elijah the great prophet of fire it was at the last not in the fire, and not in the whirlwind, but 'in a sound of gentle stillness' – with a still, small voice – that God spoke. Those who resist Him He will ultimately break in pieces, but on those who fear His Name He will rise with healing in His wings.

I am grateful to those who have allowed me to use their testimonies and other spoken or written contributions; particular thanks are due to Kenny Borthwick and Allan Wiggins. I am indebted to my wife Isobel, my daughter Mary and Jennifer Jack, for their proofreading labours and advice (whether taken or not!). As for authorship, my daughter Dr Alison Black has undertaken a large part of the work of turning a great deal of raw material into a book, although first-person references in the main text are to myself.

Chapter 1

God of the Great and Small

Did Jesus say, 'Come unto me, all ye that fear spiders...?'

This was the line that caught my attention as I glanced over the sheet of paper that was handed to me at the end of our Saturday night meeting in Glasgow.[1] The writer clearly expected the answer 'no'. A Christian leader in another town, he had put out this advertisement in his own local press and had sent a complimentary copy to us, the object of his wrath.

We had been doing our own advertising, and it was evidently this that had provoked his response. On 24 August 1996 the following notice had appeared in the *Herald*:

Struthers Memorial Church
Westbourne Gardens, Hyndland
Saturdays at 7.30 pm

Recently, many people have been set free from phobias –
for example: Agoraphobia, fear of water, darkness, heights,
drowning, enclosed spaces, spiders, snakes, wasps, bees, insects
and a multitude of others.

It is openly proclaimed that almost all who come will be healed
within two minutes and the healing will be permanent; the success
rate is in fact 98% and scores of people in the gathering are able
to testify to what has happened.

If you suffer from any kind of phobia, please do come and know
the wonderful change that deliverance brings.

On the Saturday night immediately following this advertisement, the first four who received prayer for phobias were asked to testify before I proceeded with further ministry. Three of the four were unknown to me. One and all testified convincingly to having been set free, and others were encouraged until eventually a flood of people came for ministry of this and other kinds.

A second advert followed the first in the *Herald* a week later:

Saturday Nights at Struthers are Special
7:30 pm: Westbourne Gardens, Hyndland

Last Saturday there was an open demonstration of the power of God in delivering from phobias.

We have no doubt God will move again this week if people avail themselves of the opportunity.

It was not in any spirit of bombast that I had thus advertised God's power to heal phobias. No one who heard the preaching that accompanied ministry on either occasion could have any grounds to fear that phobias were usurping too high a position in the scale of spiritual priorities. But at that time God was shining a great light on fundamental principles of faith for me through this one ministry. In addition, during the immediately preceding weeks, when preaching in a variety of churches across the country, I had seen something like fifty phobias healed. And there came over my spirit the desire to throw off the gloves altogether and be very open. Hence the advertisements in the national press.

My critic's response caused me to reflect. What did Jesus say?

He said,

> *Come unto me, all ye that labour and are heavy laden, and I will give you rest. Take my yoke upon you, and learn of me; for I am meek and lowly in heart: and ye shall find rest unto your souls.* (Matthew 11:28–9)

Why is it that in certain religious circles there is forever an attempt to keep God far away? We think of God in connection with eternal salvation. That is very relevant, but it can become theoretic and remote. One thing God has taught me over the years is that He is the God of the now, the God of the daily life, the God of the common-place – not only the God of the great eternal issues, but the God of the down-to-earth issues of life.

Perhaps our critic would have been less severe had he known more of the detail that lay behind the public notices. An example is that of **Barbara**, who had found release from a phobia – of spiders, no less! – the previous year. In her testimony the spiritual and the commonplace are noticeably intertwined.

> 'O God, give me a living experience of the living Christ.'

This was Barbara's prayer one night during our August camp/conference of 1995. The words evoke the memory of the apostle John on the isle of Patmos and of the Christ at whose feet he fell as one dead. They speak of a desire for spiritual reality such as is found in time of revival.

The significant thing for our purposes is this: the answer to her prayer involved her deliverance from the fear of spiders. The way in which this happened should stand as a firm though loving reproof to any whose God is great enough to speak in the whirlwind of revival but not intimate enough to speak in a still, small voice for the reviving of the individual. As Barbara told it 24 hours later:

> Last night I was one of the people who came forward for ministry. I came because I needed to be obedient. I had a fear of spiders, and although there had been many opportunities for prayer over the last few years I had never taken advantage of them.

The fear came in when I was about 14 years of age, still living in Rhodesia (now Zimbabwe). We had moved into a home built on red soil, which we found was a natural habitat for very large spiders. I had a few nasty encounters with some of these.

For example, I remember one day putting my hand in the top shelf of my cupboard and feeling something touch me. As I looked up, there, sitting on the top of my hand and broader than the width of my bare arm, was an enormous spider. It ran down my upraised arm and swivelled round over my shoulder. Of course I screamed, and my mother came into the room and started shaking my clothes until eventually the creature fell off.

It seemed that there was instance after instance of spiders coming into that home. One day I came in from school to discover one the size of my hand, on the hem of the curtain just above my bed. My mother followed with the fly spray – the African version of which would choke you, being so potent: British brands smell like perfume in comparison. I stood in the doorway while Mum sprayed. It turned out that this was a jumping spider! It sprang on to my bed and thence to the floor. The spider and I, both in a panic, ran down the passage, which was probably about twenty feet (six metres) long – and if you could have seen the speed at which that spider ran! So vivid is the memory that I really believe this was when the fear came in. I could not believe my eyes. The spider ran down that passage in a second, while I ran out of the lounge on to the veranda. Eventually Mum called me into the house: 'Come and see it!' When a spider dies it curls up into a ball: this one was the size of a golf ball.

Even after we moved away from that home, occasionally I would find a spider in my room. On one occasion, eyeing what looked like a grey ball of fluff on the bedroom ceiling, my mother said, 'I wonder what that is?' Never having seen anything like it before, we left it undisturbed, until one day when I came home from work she said, 'I thought I'd leave things to show you what's happened.' I went into my room to find the ceiling covered in baby spiders. Knowing by this stage that I had a chronic fear of spiders, the family made no objection to my moving immediately into my brother's room! The family were always very good. They never got fed up with me; they just understood, and they were always the ones to get rid of the spiders.

Eventually I came to live in the UK. In the eight years that I have lived in this country, I have seen relatively few of the creatures. In Glasgow recently when I came across a fairly small specimen on the wall, I got the phone book – you know, it had to be a really big book! Just to approach the creature brought dread. I thought, 'I've just got to rush at this thing and kill it.' I did so but couldn't look at it. Even the phone book had to go in the bin!

Although I have encountered fewer spiders in recent years, in both Zimbabwe and the UK they have caused me many bad dreams. In a recent one, I was in a room that was suddenly covered in a spider web in which I found myself entangled. At one end of it I could see a spider on a thread, and it came running in a straight line for me. When it sat on my neck I woke up. In another frequent dream, as I lay in bed I would look up and see a spider on the ceiling. Inevitably the creature would fall off on top of me!

I'll not describe all my dreams. But for a couple of years we have been encouraged to come forward to have prayer for phobias. Though I knew I had a fear, since the dreams hadn't been too frequent I tended to think, 'If I have another dream, then I'll see about it.'

During the camp week, as she listened to Pauline Anderson's teaching on phobias, Barbara became convicted of sin in her refusal to respond.[2] And that, she says, is how God started prompting her.

> The Holy Spirit was very gracious. The way He spoke to me was this: 'If someone came and told you that Jesus Christ was in the meeting hall and was taking away fears and healing people, and if He knew that you were in your room with that fear, and you didn't come, what disrespect that would be! Wouldn't that be an insult to Christ?'
>
> 'Yes,' I thought, 'it would. It's time I was obedient.'
>
> I didn't feel that I was living very close to Christ, but I was very open at a deep level, though unsure what to expect.

In giving the call for ministry later that week, I urged those seeking help not to delay. That was when Barbara got out of her seat and came forward. She describes what happened when Alison Speirs came to pray for her.[3]

> 'Why are you here?' asked Alison.
>
> 'I have had a fear of spiders for a very long time,' I said, but did not mention the nightmares.
>
> We prayed in tongues together, and it was not long before I was lying on the floor. I spoke quietly in tongues for some time and actually took my mind off the reason I had come forward for ministry. There came to my memory the last sentence of the sermon: 'Ask Him to be your wonderful counsellor, your mighty God, your everlasting Father, and your Prince of Peace.'[4] I said, 'O God, be my wonderful counsellor, my mighty God, my everlasting Father, and my Prince of Peace. And please take away these bad dreams of spiders, and take away the fear.'
>
> From the other side of the curtain I could hear the congregation singing, 'O hallelujah, Thou art so lovely and fair!' And I began to go into the Spirit. Lifting up my hands in worship, I began singing along with the

others. A love for Christ came into my heart, and I started to cry. Alison encouraged me, saying, 'Yes, Barbara, just go into worship.' It was a very deep worship, and I was aware of a need to cry. The congregation were continuing to sing, 'O hallelujah, Thou art so lovely and fair.' And God revealed Christ to me. As the congregation were singing I saw Christ in the open air, and I was aware of animals coming towards Him: mostly large, of many different species. Having been on safari, I know the beauty of them. I was aware that these animals were coming towards Christ, that they knew that He was the Son of God, and that He was 'so lovely and fair' to them.

God's little creatures

I began to weep, and as I was aware of Christ being there, I was also aware that although all these animals were coming to Him, His attention was on something on the ground – the smallest creature there. Then I saw the spider coming towards Christ, and He knelt down, and He reached out ... and the spider reached Him ... and He took it up in His hand. And I felt just how safe that spider was in Christ's hand. During the service I had prayed, 'O God, give me a living experience of the living Christ.' As it came to the point where the spider met Christ, I became aware of the deep, deep peace that was in Christ. There was no fear in Him. As He held the spider in His hand, there was such an immense peace. It was His creature, and He was the Lord of the heaven and the earth.

In that moment the picture seemed to change, and I saw that in both of His hands there were many small spiders. I suddenly became aware of the count-less spiders that I had killed over the years. A deep grief welled up inside me, so painful that I wanted to cry out loud. Tears were rolling down my cheeks – and immediately I heard myself screaming, pausing only long enough at intervals to draw breath. But what I was feeling was grief. It was like two things happening at once: knowing a burden of grief within, and yet being aware of screaming.

At this point Diana Rutherford ministered to Barbara, encouraging her to go quietly into tongues and be under the control of the Holy Spirit:

Diana used the words 'God's little creatures'. It was wonderfully appropriate, and I hadn't spoken to her.

I am really grateful that it has happened, and amazed that God had something for me at this camp. It has been said that camp is a divine appointment, and it certainly was so for me. I will never forget what I experienced last night.

Aftermath

The months passed, and I did not hear anything further on the subject from Barbara until Christmas of the following year, when I received a letter from her. In it she described how her new-found freedom was tested:

I really wanted to share with you that in fifteen months since, I have not had one dream of spiders.

This is not something I have talked about even to friends because Jesus has been such a close companion and it has been enough to thank Him and share with Him. However, I thought it would interest you and I wanted to tell you personally.

From the time of deliverance I knew a real difference within myself and felt much closer to Christ.

She explained how she had waited for the miracle to be fully revealed:

Months passed and one Thursday morning (August 1996) there was a large spider in my bath. By Saturday noon it was still there, it had not budged. I did not take a bath for two and a half days. I wasn't afraid, but I hoped it would go away on its own. However, it reached a time when I really wanted a bath. I approached the bath rather hesitantly and then knelt down beside it. Somehow my arm went into the bath and the spider moved nervously. To my surprise I heard myself speaking tenderly to it, 'Don't be alarmed, I'm going to help you' ... and as I spoke like this I felt a peace touch me from my head to my feet, and I lifted the spider and carried it slowly and laid it softly on the window ledge outside. I stepped back and stood still; the peace was something tangible. Then there came a knowledge into my spirit that not a trace of fear had touched me. For over 20 years I couldn't bear to be around when someone else would be asked to get rid of a spider.

This incident happened just a few days before August camp last year, so it was a blessing to go back to Craigie exactly a year since receiving ministry for the phobia, knowing the total absence of bad dreams in that year and also knowing how completely the fear had gone concerning spiders.

The peace of Christ that had touched Barbara so profoundly as she lay on the floor at the earlier August camp had come to stay, and now she was sure of it. Years later she said that not only had the miracle remained, but a new love for Christ had sprung from it, bringing about a transformation of attitudes in other areas.

The New Ministry

The reader may possibly be wondering what 'lying on the floor' had to do with Barbara's healing. In fact many phobias are removed in a couple of minutes as the sufferer sits to receive prayer.[5] Barbara's healing, however, was one of a wide range of experiences flowing from a 'new ministry' in our churches. There had come upon me in November 1994 an anointing under which many went prostrate as they received prayer. Within a matter of weeks a number of others in our movement entered into the same ministry. Although prostration was a frequent outward sign of this new wave of the Spirit, there was an inner significance as well. The individual was brought into very direct touch with the Spirit of God. At times little or no human ministry was involved. Sometimes just the words 'the anointing of the holy' were all that were spoken in prayer. The person was on God's operating table – and the divine surgeon conducted His own operation. The needs of the body as well as those of the mind and spirit were addressed. This book, like its predecessors, indicates something of the variety of this ministry of the Spirit.[6]

The Significance of Phobias

Phobias may be a small matter – but they can be very important if they keep you from the fullness of God. Very often the thing that lies between the soul and God is a very small matter. It is almost like a veiling, a gossamer covering that comes between you and God, but it is enough to blur the outlook, to cloud the relationship with God. Christ came that we might have life and that we might have it abundantly – and yet I find that very few Christians are enjoying abundant life. They may be keeping their heads above water, but they are not really all that happy. They are striving and struggling, and there is not that deep soul unity with God. They are not living under a cloudless sky.

Hudson Taylor's wife Maria in dying could say that for the last ten years she had never known a shadow between her soul and Christ: an endless living in the light of God without a shadow, without a turmoil of the kind that is within nearly all Christian lives. It is when you counsel people who come for help that you begin to realize the vast number of issues that come between the soul and God. Often the issues are comparatively small. People will say to me, 'I hardly like to bring this, it seems so trivial.' They are mentally comparing their situation, perhaps, with that of someone dying of cancer – and here they have come with a phobia that doesn't amount to a great deal. But why carry it? Why put up with it? I have discovered in dealing with phobias that one is dealing not just with the phobia itself. When the phobia is removed there comes an upwelling, a springing up of life. Many other things tend to vanish along with the main phobia, and the person comes into a place of release and joy and fullness.

Although I was quite definite on the subject of God's willingness to heal phobias (advertisements to the contrary notwithstanding!), there nevertheless were questions that had already occurred to my own mind about the relation between the particular moving of God in our midst and His moving in revival power in our own land in the past, or in places such as Mexico in the present. We were aware of the diversity of the Spirit's operations in many places at this time, often through first-hand reports. A snapshot of the Mexican revival was brought to us by a friend who found himself unexpectedly involved in it. His story is recorded in the next chapter.

Notes

1. The Saturday night meeting, now held in the church in Westbourne Gardens, Glasgow, is the largest of our weekly gatherings. It is attended by many visitors from various denominations and none, some travelling the length of the country to be there. God manifests His presence there regularly.

2. Pauline Anderson appears in chapter 3 as well as in several of my other books. See, for example, *The Incomparable Christ* (New Dawn Books, 1989), Part 2.

3. For Alison Speirs's story, see my *Revival: Personal Encounters* (New Dawn Books, 1993). Alison's own accounts of the new ministry are related in the first two books of this series, *A View from the Floor* (chapter 8) and *Further Views from the Floor* (chapter 3). Both books were published by New Wine Press in 1997.

4. The speaker was Jennifer Jack. She is featured in various of my books, e.g. *Consider Him: The Qualities of Christ* (New Dawn Books, 1988), Part 2 and *Further Views from the Floor*, chapters 2–3.
5. See Appendix for an explanation of how deliverance from phobias takes place.
6. For these matters, see *A View from the Floor* and *Further Views from the Floor*.

Chapter 2

Revival in Mexico

In Barbara's story we saw how wonderfully Christ can be revealed in the seemingly small things of life. The present chapter describes the moving of God on a much larger scale where thousands were affected – and it tells what it was like for one young man who found himself in the midst of it. **Allan Wiggins** was an ordained, Spirit-filled minister with the Assemblies of God when he went on a preaching mission to Mexico.[1] A gifted evangelist who was used to seeing the miraculous in his ministry, he encountered in Mexico something unexpectedly different. If there had been any thought of self-sufficiency before he arrived, it fled far away in the tumultuous dealing of God with his own life in the midst of that revival.

Not long before Allan left this country on the journey that took him to Mexico, he had already had a meeting with God. For some time I had felt a need in his life and had been dropping hints about it. I said, 'Come, we'll pray.' We went upstairs and prayed sitting; then I asked him to stand. He told me later that he never goes prostrate – but he went down immediately. And suddenly there came a flash of an incident when I had prayed with him a number of months earlier, and with the memory he became aware that there was fear in him. He said as he went down it was as though a chain broke inside him, and he was set free.

In April 1995 he gave a report on his Mexican visits:

> I have been asked to speak about revival in Mexico. The fact of the matter is that everywhere in the 'two-thirds' world there are pockets of revival. Yet in the western hemisphere we've got dry bones. This was brought home to me by a car sticker I saw in the States. It said: 'If God fails to judge San Francisco, then He must apologize to Sodom and Gomorrah.' Looking at that sticker made me realize the condition the western world is in.

Alluding to the oft-cited injunction of a founder of the Struthers movement, Allan continued:

> For the first time ever in my life it has been very difficult to speak, because this revival is so pure and so holy, and Miss Taylor's words are exactly right: **Get right before God before revival comes – because you won't find it easy when it does.**[2] I know that for a fact.
>
> My previous three visits to the States in the past year were spent ministering in big meetings. This time was a bit different because I was going to be doing a lot of street work in the ghettos with alcoholics, drug addicts and prostitutes. Mexico was a kind of afterthought. Before going to the States I had come through absolute hell on earth with the devil, and after a conversation with Mr Black I became convinced that we were going to see a move of God. My two girls had come down with chicken-pox. My wife had a serious operation; then two days before my departure she broke her toe. The company that booked my ticket lost all record of me in the computer; a courier delivered my tickets a couple of days before the flight. So I knew that there would be a move of God, and I took it that it would just be the same as the last couple of times I had been there. I would be preaching in big meetings, and we would see a lot of people saved,

healed and baptized in the Holy Ghost. That was why I was going: to preach the gospel and ask God to demonstrate His kingdom. I did not for a minute think that I would see revival. There are many people like this today. We pray for revival, and we say how much we want revival – but do you really believe that we're going to see it in this generation? There have been times in my life when I have felt the church, myself included, was too far gone.

But I was to go down to Mexico, only half-an-hour's drive from where we were staying in California. That Wednesday I noticed that I just wanted to be on my own and pray. For three hours in my room I prayed and read the Word. I was groaning in my spirit, without knowing why. This lasted until I was physically weak, and my hostess came to give me a meal.

As we were going down to Mexico in the car, one of my companions who knew me said, 'You're very quiet.'

'Well, I'm deep in thought.'

'Are you nervous?'

'Don't be so stupid! Nervous? I'm **terrified**! Not even the Americans can understand me [because of my Scots accent]; how are these Mexicans going to interpret for me?'

There were two pastors with us, one of whom had asked me after I had been ministering in his church the previous morning, 'How does it feel to preach in a Christian country?'

I said, 'I'll let you know when I come back from Mexico.' America is not a Christian country. (What kind of Christian country does not allow its children to pray in schools?) It needs revival.

This pastor warned me, 'These Mexicans are very uneducated, so you will have to preach a simple message.'

I don't know what else to preach anyway, but I said to him, 'They can't be too far uneducated.'

'Why?'

'Well, I'm going to speak in English, and one of them is going to interpret into Spanish. Can you speak two languages? You can't even speak the Queen's English properly!'

Despite the banter, Allan was thoughtful. He had already felt the devil on his back. And now he wondered if it was true that these uneducated people would not know the things of God as deeply as their more affluent neighbours.

Then a more pressing problem interrupted his meditations. He and his companions were over the Mexican border by this time, following the signs for the airport, as instructed – but it became clear that they were heading in the wrong direction. The road signs seemed not to make sense. Another kind of sign proved more helpful, however:

We eventually found a road and knew as we were going up it that this was where the meeting was, because we could feel the presence of God. Reaching the top of the road we saw the church in the distance. It was a warehouse (the only people who have church buildings in Mexico are Roman Catholics). I felt, 'This is holy ground we are driving on.' I was beginning to get convicted of sin, and it was in my own life. As we drove up we could hear the singing in Spanish and the clapping of hands. Some Mexicans were waiting outside, because we were late by this time.

I got out of the car, and a little Mexican shouted at me:

'Pastor Wiggly, Pastor Wiggly, we're glad to see you! Come in!'

The hot wind of God

They took me into the building. The best way to describe this is to say it was as if I was hit by the hot wind of God.

'I've never been in a meeting like this,' I thought. 'It must be because they speak in a different language.'

I sat on the platform watching. It was evidently getting near the time to preach, because they were mentioning my name and had already fitted me with the radio mike. I was going to preach from Acts chapter two. My notes were all set out – sharp notes, for the interpreter's benefit – and I felt the Lord speak to my spirit. 'Your notes on Acts chapter two are going to be no good to you tonight. You are on holy ground. You are on new ground that you have never experienced before. I want you to preach from Mark 16, the great commission.'

If I had been terrified coming through the door, I was even more terrified now by the fact that I was speaking in English and a guy was interpreting in Spanish to a crowd that I didn't know. But the glory and the presence of God fell upon me, and the best way to describe it is this. It manifests itself in the anointing. The anointing of God is the manifest presence of God, and I could feel God very, very close. I was overcome by His holiness – and my filthy rags. I was convicted of sin. When I thought about it afterwards, it struck me that the sin I was convicted of was this: I had read the O.J. Simpson trial in the newspaper that morning before I had looked at my Bible. Back here in Scotland that's just a trifling affair; it is normal for many a churchgoer to read the newspaper before reading the Bible. But I was convicted of this. It was as if I had committed murder: such was the conviction of sin that I'd never felt before, not even at conversion nor during my baptism in the Holy Ghost. I was totally overcome. Standing up to speak at one stage I did not feel able to preach to this congregation, many of whom were still on their feet and speaking.

'What's going on here?' I asked the Mexican pastor.

'These people are being healed,' he said. 'We'll have some of their testimonies later.'

This was blowing my mind!

Eventually I started to preach from Mark 16. People were standing up. There was an anointing on the ministry that had previously only been there in little spurts, and I knew then that I was in revival, and that revival is one hundred per cent of God and none of man. I knew then that Duncan Campbell and Mr Black and those who had been in the Lewis revival had met with the living God in a personal way. The awesomeness and holiness of God was overpowering. And of course when God manifests Himself in that way, signs and wonders occur.

The Lord was speaking to me as I was preaching. He said that this revival was not for one denomination or for one movement, but that it would go through the denominations and through the movements, and that God would share His glory with no man. That is why I have found it very difficult to speak: God would share His glory with no man. It was frightening.

People started running to the altar as I was preaching, crying their eyes out under conviction of sin. You see, in revival they had a choice: they could either run to the altar or they could run out of the door. Many people in the west have run out of the door when revival comes. But these Mexicans were running to the altar.

Alcoholics were coming in off the street and getting sobered up and giving their heart to Jesus as the preaching continued.

Two prostitutes came running in the church door. Thinking they were about to attack me, I was ready with my big Bible to whack the two of them! If you have read my testimony in *The Baptism in the Spirit and Its Effects* you will know a similar story! I don't tolerate devils lightly today. But the two girls came in weeping, and they threw their money down in front of the altar and lay on the floor crying their eyes out to God. They were shouting, '*Cristo te ama, Cristo te ama, Cristo te ama!*' That means, 'Jesus loves you.' These were two girls who had been out on the street five minutes earlier with two men. They came right in that door and they lay there.

By this time, there would probably be two or three hundred people at the altar, and I was still preaching.

I said to Pastor Rigo, 'Do you want me to stop preaching and go and lay hands on these people?'

He said to me, 'This is not X_____: this is Mexico. In X_____ they've cut down on the preaching of the gospel. In Mexico we've been denied the preaching of the gospel for too long, and we're certainly not going to cut down on it. You'll preach for another thirty minutes!' It was all right for this guy: he was used to the revival! My knees were knocking – I was sweating with conviction of sin – and he was telling me to preach for another half hour!

'What do I preach on, Lord?'

'Just keep going.'

God spoke again in my spirit, telling me to speak out in words of knowledge. These were not of the type that we often hear in the west ('There's someone here with arthritis' – half of Greenock has arthritis!) but specific words for specific people. One in particular I'll never forget. It was for a well-dressed man sitting to one side of me. I thought at first he was a pastor, but during the preaching I noticed that he was not right with God – not because of the way he looked, but because it was a supernatural realm in which I was seeing.

The Lord had me say to him, 'Your drug dealing will become your addiction if you walk out that door without Christ.'

He was a drug dealer in Mexico, and he almost had a heart attack while he was sitting there. That guy came to the altar.

Then as the preaching continued I had a revelation that there was someone healed directly behind the Scottish people who were with me. I asked the person concerned to stand up, and when he did so, the audience started to clap their hands and stamp on the floor, rising to their feet as the guy came to the altar. I couldn't tell what was going on, because it was in Spanish.

Pastor Rigo said to me, 'You don't know this man.'

I said, 'No.'

He said, 'This man is a blind beggar on the streets of Tijuana. But he's no longer blind: he sees!'

And Rigo was still wanting me to preach for another fifteen minutes after that! By this time I was overwhelmed by the power, the awesomeness, the grace, the majesty, and the judgment arm of God. Those people coming to that altar were under judgment. But they left it under grace, because they gave their hearts to Christ. I tell you, that judgment and that type of meeting are coming.

How do I know it was revival, and not just a blessing? That's simple. Four weeks ago, Rigo, the pastor, had a church of 50 people. An American pastor went there and it went to 150 in one week. By the time I got to Rigo's church there were 1,000. I left it on the Wednesday and when I got back on the Friday it was closed, and the Mexicans were waiting on me.

'Pastor Wiggly, Pastor Wiggly, the church has moved!'

I thought, 'I hope Rigo's moved, because I don't want to be preaching for an hour and a half again!'

'Where has it moved?'

'It's moved further up the road. We've bought a building for 3,000 people.' And the American pastor who was with me said, 'Why did you buy a building for 3,000? We only had 1,000 on Wednesday! That place is going to be half empty! How do you think this Scotsman's going to feel in a half-empty Mexican church?'

I'd have felt at home, because most of the churches I've preached in are half empty! – and dead! So I wasn't too bothered. But the Mexicans said to him, 'No, there have been 4,000 in the meeting since six o'clock. Pastor Wiggly not to preach till 7:30.'

So there were 4,000 gathered at six o'clock for the best seats for their healing. That's why we know it's revival. One of the most satisfying things about it for me was the fact that when these people were coming to Christ they were throwing their icons in the bin. It was a big bin, and into it went the statues, the beads and the indulgences, as we prayed that Jesus would set them free from all this religion that had bound them up.

The testimonies in that church are absolutely amazing. The city of Tijuana is being fired up for God through this. There is a move in the established church there to come against these Christians, but Rigo (who must have been a bandit before he was a pastor!) said to me, 'These gringos don't understand. God will close their churches before He'll close mine! – because I'm taking all their people!' And so he was. He was taking them by the hundreds, and people were coming under deep conviction of sin.

On their return to California, events took an unexpected turn:

He was right. One day we were in a restaurant in San Diego. Outside the restaurant were four TV crews

The American pastor had said to me, 'It's no good being in revival if you don't take it with you. There's no point leaving it in Mexico!'

filming a guy who was standing speaking on a platform. His theme was, 'Save San Diego bay from
pollution, and save the whales, and save the ecology,
and save everything.'

The pastor said to me, 'Is that fire exit opened?'

I said, 'Yes.'

He said, 'Well, as soon as that guy steps down,
we're going up there to speak.'

I said, 'You're not on! Four TV crews? I've spoken
on the telly before – it's murder!'

He said, 'We're going on there. Do you believe that
revival touched you?'

'Yes, I do.'

'Well, get up there and witness for Jesus.'

The two of us walked out. The other guy who was
with us by this time was in a state of shock. When the
speaker had finished, the pastor walked up and said,
'Thank you, ladies and gentlemen, for coming – and
save the whale, and save the bay, and save everything
else. But I want to tell you something. Jesus Christ is
the answer to your souls! He'll save your soul! And
more than that, I've brought a Scotsman here from
Scotland to tell you about it!'

It was broadcast on the San Diego news that there
were two Scotsmen and an American preaching the
gospel during a campaign to save the whale! I
wouldn't have had the guts or the bottle to do that,
even though I am quite up front.

In retrospect Allan felt that the episode in San Diego
owed more to human zeal than to the genuine urge of the
Spirit. But, as he explains,

We saw so many unusual things happening. I had
moved into a supernatural realm in the anointing of
God that I did not think was possible for me. God
has done many things in my life over a short number
of years. I was expecting to see thousands of people

saved when I went to America, because God had never let me down on earlier occasions. But I was not expecting to meet with Him in revival power – and it frightened the living daylights out of me. My message to the church is this: get right before Him. When you get right before Him, sinners will come through the door because they will be under conviction of sin. Those prostitutes didn't just walk in the door non-chalantly. They came running. The drunks came running, because they were convicted of sin right where they were. That day is coming. But the church has to be right to meet them. That is where we have to get ourselves right with God.

Addressing our own congregation, Allan observed:

I hope that a fire has been lit up in your hearts, because you're a church that very much believes in God for revival. Keep believing Him, for it will come. Our nation needs revival. It needs a touch of God more than most nations because we have gone so far back. But God hasn't finished with Great Britain, and the Christians can play their part in it.

There are people here under the same conviction of sin. I have felt the same presence of God with me while walking down that aisle. When God touches you in revival it stays. And I noticed when Mr Black was speaking earlier that people were becoming convicted of sin. That is a good sign for the church of Jesus Christ. God wants you, as Miss Taylor rightly said, to get right with Him before the revival does come – because you'll be feeling inadequate enough without having ongoing sin in your life. God wants to touch so many lives here, including my own. I believe my life has been touched just coming here to share this with you. It's the most difficult thing I've had to speak about in my life. Normally for me to come and speak is no problem. But when you are speaking about the awesome holiness of God, it just overwhelms you. When I came off the plane from America, people saw a difference in me. My wife saw it, and various people in Greenock said to me, 'There's something different.' It is the Shekinah glory of God, I believe, that has fallen on some of us.

The awesome meeting with God that Allan describes was something that I could well understand. As a congregation we were aware of this side of the character of God, and in the present moving of His Spirit there were those who experienced Him in something of this way, as the next chapter shows.

Notes

1. For an absorbing account of Allan's conversion from a life of alcoholism, see *The Baptism in the Spirit and Its Effects* (New Dawn Books, 1994), Part 2.

2. 'Easy' in the sense of 'comfortable'. The words are a paraphrase of a sentiment occasionally voiced by the late Elizabeth H. Taylor. For her story, see Part 2 of my book *A Trumpet Call to Women*. For her teachings and other relevant material, see *E.H. Taylor: A Modern Christian Mystic*, compiled and edited by Hugh B. Black (New Dawn Books, 1994).

Chapter 3

The Awe of God

There was one of our company whose testimony touched the particular note of the fear of God – the sense of the divine. This was **Pauline**, who described her encounter in *A View from the Floor*.

Although she had ministered fruitfully to others she had felt no particular need or urge to seek ministry for herself. She had ultimately asked for it not out of any overwhelming compulsion to do so, but as an 'experiment' – just in case God should have something for her. She recapitulated it for us on the same night on which Allan testified:

Turning to prayer, I had no idea what was going to happen. But as we prayed, an almighty power of God came down upon me. I felt as if I was falling, not backwards, but forwards, though still on my feet. It was like falling and falling down into blackness. It was very different from other wonderful-sounding experiences of tremendous light and love. Although this was not terrifying in any way, it was just like going down into a sheer and utter blackness. It came to a point when the power that had come upon me was so awesome I could not stand, and I collapsed in a very undignified heap on the floor.

As I fell, what really struck me was that the God who was in that blackness was awesome. There was an awesomeness of the presence of God that I had never known in my life, whether in salvation, baptism in the Spirit, or even deliverance. Though deliverance had been an awesome experience, it wasn't like this. One could not trifle with this God. Two words came into my mind: **sin** and **hell**. I thought, 'Sin takes a man to hell.' It's not as though God puts a man or a woman in hell: sin takes them to hell; there's nowhere else for them. There are people who blaspheme the Name of Christ and are very glib and blasé about what they would do to God, and so on. The world is in for an immense shock. When people die they will confront the awesomeness of this God. I felt Him speak to my own life.

When I got up from that experience, the sense of awe remained. I was like a zombie for the next twenty-four hours or so. I went home feeling I couldn't talk to anybody. Living alone, I was glad that there was nobody in; glad that there were no messages on the answering machine; glad that I had the whole of the next day to myself. As I walked the streets in a daze, there kept going through my mind **the awesomeness of God**.

Pauline's story had an interesting sequel, not hitherto published:

When Mr Black asked me to share my testimony that night in Greenock, I thought, 'How am I going to be able to do that?' But God came. After that something of the weight of it lifted. But things weren't complete. Something had still to happen. Though the darkness had not been terrifying, I did not know what it was. The next night, after the open ministry in the Glasgow meeting, I was drawn to go forward again. This time it was completely different, but lovely. Instead of going down into a blackness, I was aware at first of my head going forwards; then there came down the light that I associate with resurrection. There was the sense of resurrection life and light pouring down upon me. My head went right up as though facing the light pouring from above. There came a point again when I could not stand. Whereas on the previous occasion the sheer power of God had brought me to my knees, this time it was as if I had no energy and just went right back. The feeling of resurrection – that's the only way I can put it – came pouring into my body. As I lay there all my limbs were shaking uncontrollably. I thought, 'I can't stop this.' Let it be quite clear that I am not normally given to shaking! It has happened only once or twice before: at my baptism in the Spirit, and then a week later when I felt the overflow of power after praying with someone. But here I lay unable to stop shaking. And so I just let it take its course.

But the crux of it is this. The moment I got up off the floor, I knew what had happened. God had not revealed it a minute beforehand nor on the Friday night. But when I got up He showed me that the blackness that I had fallen into signified the death of an inner part. I knew what part it was. For years I had known that God needed to do something at a deep level. I had been as faithful and given as much as I could, but the work was not complete. And in those moments God showed me that something had died. It was vital that it die. That blackness was the going down into death – and the light that came was resurrection light. There was a rising up again and leaving the old part behind.

That was about seven or eight weeks ago. If the proof of the pudding is in the eating, it has stood the test of those seven or eight weeks. The work that God did has subsequently gone even deeper, and I am tremendously grateful.

I was just conducting an experiment – but what an experiment it turned out to be!

There were others who spoke of experiencing the awe of God as they lay on the floor. One was **Carol S**, whose life as a young person had been radically transformed by Christ a number of years earlier. A member of our branch church in Cumbernauld, in February 1995 Carol described how she had recently met God in a new way. She had already received ministry on several occasions in our Greenock church, and found her spiritual appetite whetted for more of God, as she explained to her own minister, Diana Rutherford.[1] She describes what happened from then on:

I think that going down under the Spirit gave me a great hunger and a great desire to meet God in a deeper and a more real way. One night in Greenock I went to Diana after the meeting and said that I didn't want anything artificial about meeting God in this way – not that there was anything artificial in what I had received, but I really wanted to meet God and to know the reality of God. After my speaking to her, she agreed to pray with me the next morning in Cumbernauld.

Into the meeting there came the holy atmosphere of God – that deep, deep presence of the awesomeness of God – and the power of God began to fall. I began to enter into that, and then Diana came over and said, 'The time is right: come and let's pray.' We went out to the side and she began to pray with me. It was my intention that morning not to go down until I knew that God had put me down, until I knew, if you like, the Holy Spirit had forced me down. And I was very open to meeting God in that way; it wasn't as if I was going to have any qualms about being put down.

We prayed, and I remember Diana saying to me, 'Breathe in the stillness of God.' Quietening my spirit I breathed in deeply. And in a moment I felt something touch me inside. It was tangible: I could feel it. And in a moment I responded, completely opening up to the deepest part of my being and knowing that this power of God was real and that it was beginning to move in my life. As we prayed, waves of the power and the fire of God kept coming and coming. And I went out further and further, right out into God.

Something of the supernatural touched my life that day. At the end of it I was reminded of Moses going up Mount Sinai to meet with a holy God, a God of power, a God of fire. I do believe that was the God I met that morning; that was the God who touched my life. From that moment there has opened up an access into the presence of God that I did not know existed. The tremendous thing about it is that every time I close my eyes it's there! Every time I close my eyes that power begins to fall; the access into that glory begins to come.

There was another time a week later when the meeting began to take the same direction. I felt the holiness fall and the atmosphere of the power of God begin to open up again. Diana came over and said, 'Let's pray.' Again we went out into the aisle and prayed.

At this point in her narrative Carol drew attention to the actual experience of falling, which in one respect was reminiscent of Pauline's. She could remember nothing about the previous occasion other than that she

just fell like a sack of potatoes down on the floor. There was no choosing, which way will I fall, where will I go, what will I do? ... just *whoosh*, right down. Now on one of the occasions when I had gone out in the church in Greenock, Mr Black had said something about not resisting God. And as Diana prayed with me for the second time in Cumbernauld I really didn't want to resist God in any way; I wanted to be as obedient to the Holy Spirit as I possibly could. But I wanted to wait until the last possible moment, until

God put me down. Again the waves of His power began to fall. I went with it and I went down, but again it wasn't a kind of choosing to go down: it was just, 'Oof, I can't stand here any more, I must go down!' And down I went.

It was absolutely beautiful what happened. I fell into the silence of light. These are the only words to describe what I experienced. I was out in the presence of God. I was not aware of the meeting or of anyone other than Diana, who was beside me. I was just aware of the silence of the light of God.

That experience showed me that Christ has reconciled us to God: Christ has opened up the way for us to enter in. What is burning in my mind is that this ministry is not only bringing healing and other wonderful things for our lives, but it is opening up a way for us to go into the presence of God. Those words have been burning: 'Enter in. Enter into that presence of God.' God has not to my knowledge done anything with me physically. But I praise Him because He has allowed me the privilege of entering in at a deep level to the presence of the Most High. Praise His Name.

Another of our members, **Linda J**, kept a diary from which she later compiled the following notes on three separate encounters with God.[2] She writes:

The new ministry came into the church at a time when I was seeking God in a deeper way than I had ever sought Him before. A realization had dawned upon my spirit that after being a Christian for over twenty-five years, a deeper seeking for God was necessary and desirable.

The verses of Scripture which were burning in my heart at that time, and even more so today, were: *Oh that I knew where I might find him! that I might come even to his seat!* (Job 23:3) and *ye shall seek me, and*

*find me, when ye shall search for me with all your heart.
And I will be found of you, saith the LORD* (Jeremiah
29:13–14).

The ensuing events followed a time of deep repentance for sin, wrong decisions and wrong reactions.
Seeking for God in a deeper way brought about
conviction of sin and repentance, succeeded by a time
of rich blessing.

Linda received ministry in January 1995:

Over the past months I had been struggling with
anxiety and fear about being alone. If I was on my
own would I be able to cope with feelings of isolation
and aloneness? I knew that Christ is our 'nearest
kinsman' and my dearest friend, but I had a gnawing
fear about being alone. I knew that I should be
content if I had Jesus only, and I desired that this
should be so.

During the Sunday evening service in Cumbernauld, Diana Rutherford opened the meeting for
ministry. I went forward, and as we prayed I came
through in spirit into what seemed a large bright
place. I was brought by angelic presence before the
great white throne. It was awesome. There was an
awareness that the period of conviction of sin and
repentance had permitted this deeper access to the
throne of God. It would have been impossible to
stand in this presence. The fear of aloneness left me,
and it was replaced by a certainty that Jesus would
never leave me nor forsake me.

Linda's desire for God continued to deepen. In February she went forward for ministry again:

As we prayed I became aware of an awesome
presence. I was surrounded by what felt like rich
velvet, and I was aware of the power of Jehovah God.

Again, it would have been impossible to stay standing. The power was so intense that I felt I could not stand it, and I almost asked Diana to stop praying with me. I knew I wanted more of God, so I entered into what God was doing in my life. I felt that the Holy Spirit had opened up a well within me. It was clean and pure. It is so difficult to explain, but it was as if part of my old life had been sealed up and something new had replaced it. A new well had been dug deep within and filled with pure, clear water. Something new had happened in spiritual places.

The God who cared for the needs of Linda's spirit also met the needs of her mind and body, when she sought ministry in our Glasgow church one night in May of the same year:

I went out for ministry, primarily to seek prayer for healing for a painful shoulder. Pauline Anderson prayed with me, and I was set free from a fear of wasps and bees. It was a wonderful release. It happened in seconds. My shoulder was not healed immediately, but the pain eased off within a day or two.

To return to a point raised by Carol's testimony, a number of our people had wondered whether they should remain standing as long as they could and not go down until very manifestly pushed down by God. On the subject 'to fall or not to fall', I gave the following advice:

There are two dangers. On one hand there are those who come expecting to go down, and as they lean back on their heels they are halfway down already. Some who receive prayer, on the other hand, can be almost staggering, taking steps backward in order to prevent themselves from going down. Now I think that is totally wrong. You should respond to the Holy

Spirit, and in the physical realm as in the spiritual realm all that should be needed is the touch of God. The moment He indicates that He wants you on your back you should respond to His pressure. Don't fight. Indeed, if I am praying with you, and I find that you're fighting, I am quite liable to leave you to it. React to the first touch of the Holy Spirit. That doesn't mean that you fall down at the first touch. But from the moment you sense His pressure to go down, obey Him: *Whatsoever He saith unto you, do it.* When the servants who were given that instruction heard Him say, 'Fill the firkins with water,' they were not expected to stand back and say, 'I'm not going to do that until He forces me to do it.' I advise you to respond immediately when the real touch of God comes on you. That is my considered opinion, having watched quite a number of you going through a variety of processes.

But sit on the floor if you wish, when you feel the touch of God, and let Him put you back: make it easy for yourself! Get rid of all thought of the body, and go out into the deeps of God.

Notes

1. Diana Rutherford's association with the 'new ministry' is described in *A View from the Floor*, chapters 2 and 9, and *Further Views from the Floor*, chapters 7 and 8. In the latter chapter Diana contributes her own description of Carol's experience (without naming her).
2. Linda's deliverance from a phobia of fire is recorded in my book *Christ the Deliverer* (New Dawn Books, 1991), chapter 2.

Chapter 4

The Question of Revival

As I observed the manifold working of God in our midst, it seemed almost as though there were two movements going on at the same time. On the one hand He had been touching lives very sweetly and gently, as indicated by many whose testimonies are recorded in this series of books. On the other hand, in Pauline's testimony for example, there were inklings of something awe-inspiring.

Since November 1994 we had been experiencing something quite unique and special. At the same time as God had moved in His own particular way for us, there was occurring a dispensation of blessing on the wider Christian scene. Yet I noticed that many of the leaders across the country, men who really knew God, were not referring to the wave that was current in many places as 'revival'. They tended to refer to it as 'times of refreshing from the presence of the Lord', and I think in that they were very wise. Some of us are well aware, through having experienced revival or having studied it, that there is a fairly cataclysmic movement of God that can come, a movement so deep and profound that whole communities may be touched and a whole generation affected by the power of it. On the very streets there can be such a God-consciousness that people are awed and hushed, and swearing stops.

Although we were not seeing that in any great measure

in this country at the time of which I write, this did not mean that God had changed His position on historic revival. But there come times of refreshing from the presence of the Lord; and I think He had found a generation that was so far from Him (unlike the Hebrides of the 1930s and 1940s), a generation that in many cases had so little knowledge of the living God, that He came very gently, very sweetly, and very kindly.

And I found that I was drawn in two directions. I was aware on one hand of the deep moving of revival that God will bring upon His church – such a moving as appeared to be affecting Mexico just then – and I was also aware of the very sweet moving that He was currently bringing upon His church. And as I was before God I found a link between the two.

It is a very clear link, and is very simply this (as I pondered it came to me very clearly): we have nothing to do except what we are told. We have no action to take but that of response to the action of God.

> *Is this the fast that I have chosen?* (Isaiah 58:5)

God is speaking through His prophet about a human activity that focuses on external signs of repentance and humility, even lying on sackcloth and ashes, while neglecting His revealed will. He says, 'Is this what I have chosen?' No, this is what we have chosen. We can try to get revival by human action, human preparation, human sacrifice, human will worship, and by trying to obey a number of rules and principles. But this kind of human endeavour is not the road to revival. You can read the writings of Finney and say, 'Well, I'll do it just exactly the way Finney did it,' and still end up without revival – or you can move as you are moved by God.

Paul knew this secret:

> *I am crucified with Christ: nevertheless I live; yet not I, but Christ liveth in me.* (Galatians 2:20)

He reckoned himself crucified on the cross with Christ: dead to the mind, dead to the heart, dead to the will.

Such an experience actually feels like a death. Pauline spoke of how she felt like a zombie after the first of her two encounters with God. Allan told me that for about two days he was like a zombie. In an earlier day Pauline's sister Susie used very similar language when she found that God struck the will a death blow. She was like a dead person for two or three days. Remembering my own experience of this many years ago, I told her: 'Don't come out of it or hurry it up. Don't try to come back to life. Let it take its course and let God finish the operation that He begins.' It is of vital importance that we go right through into that death zone and come in God's hour into the resurrection zone. We don't rush, we don't jump.

The principle is very simple. You do what the Spirit says. If you begin to obey the Spirit He will take you from stage to stage. He may take you in gently and gradually, or He may take you in cataclysmically, but you will come ultimately to the same place if you go with the Holy Spirit. There is no formula, no blueprint. I cannot say, 'This is how it works.' God always does His own thing in His own way.

Revival is God in action through His channels, or sovereignly without His channels. He brings a God-consciousness, and He brings people into conformity with His will. While He can be very firm and conviction painful, His touch can also be very gentle and lay you down on the carpet, bless you, change you and reveal Himself to you. He can touch deeps in you that you never knew existed, heal wounds beyond your deepest knowledge of yourself. It is wonderful to go on to the operating table of the heavenly physician, who never makes a mistake in diagnosis. The best of doctors can make a mistake, and you know what has happened at times: many an appendix has come out that never needed to come out, and many another thing has happened that might have been better not happening. But when you are in the hand of God the diagnosis is perfect. There is no hesitation when He uses the surgical knife. It is precise: He never cuts any deeper than is needed, and He never inflicts unnecessary pain. He does a perfect job, with great love and gentleness and tenderness, and He makes you anew. If any man is in Christ, he is a new creature, and the more deeply you go into the hand of God the more you will be renewed.

In counselling as I have done now for most of half a century, one becomes knowledgeable about many things. But one of the things that amazes and delights me is what I hear people say when they come off the floor. I could never have taken them along certain paths. I could never have dealt with Barbara the way God did. Many who come for ministry have been counselled by me – but in a few minutes God does what I could never have done. I have counselled Pauline. I know the area to which she is referring, and it took the hand of God to bring a death and a resurrection. No human being can do that. Trust God and put your life in His hand to be changed into the great deeps.

A particularly profound and moving illustration is given in the next chapter.

Chapter 5

Heart of Revival: The Fire and the Dove

When I first returned to Greenock in November 1994 with the news of the Holy Spirit's moving at our church conference in High Wycombe, there came on some of the hearers a sense of awe. It is worth noticing that this holy fear touched some of the choicest lives in our midst: lives that were known for their ardent love for God and sacrificial service on behalf of His church. In some cases there was an admixture of human apprehension, not just of the physical experience of falling or becoming a public spectacle, but of meeting God Himself at such depth. What a great many people in fact encountered was the unutterable love of God. They found that they were clasped by the Lover of their souls. In that relationship you can go into an infinite union with Christ to go out no more, to be at one with God.

Something of the flavour of that ineffable experience is captured in the following testimony from my daughter **Grace**; it was with some reluctance that she eventually agreed to give it.[1] For those who do not know her, it is important to realize that Grace was no stranger to the love of God. An essential part of her ministry for years had lain in the communication of that love to others.

When the new ministry began in the church I was very awed by it. The first night that it happened I found that in turning to God, there came a great stillness inside. But there was accompanying it a fear which I think I have always had, and in many ways it is a good fear: *The fear of the Lord is the beginning of wisdom.* There always had been the knowledge that revival is not a comfortable thing. But I was then and over the ensuing weeks deeply moved by the way that God was working in our midst.

Though I had wanted to come for ministry, it just hadn't worked out. There had been one of our after-meetings on a Sunday night when practically all of those present had been on the floor, myself included; it had been wonderful. But I was still waiting for the right time to seek ministry.

That time came one Monday night in February 1995, during a meeting taken in Greenock by my daughter Mary.[2]

During the day I had had that kind of churned-up feeling that you sometimes have when God is going to do something particular, and I had made up my mind that if Mary gave an opportunity for ministry (which she had on the Sunday morning in Glasgow, but never on the Monday night) I would ask for it. But the Spirit began to fall on us as we were praying. There came some beautiful singing in the Spirit which led into dancing, and I discovered for the first time in my life I wanted to dance in the Spirit. Now I love it when other people dance and sing in this way, but I think as a youngster I was quite without qualification the worst dancer in the school! In our compulsory country dancing in the gymnasium, I was always the one singled out for not being in time and so on. I didn't know what I was doing wrong, but obviously it wasn't pleasing the teacher. So it had never crossed my mind that I could do such a thing.

It was quite strange. I was just sitting thinking, 'You know, I feel I could do it tonight,' when Mary came over and said to me, 'Do you not feel like dancing?' and I said, 'Yes.'

She said, 'Well, do it!'

I found myself doing it – as, I think, were others, although I was not really conscious of what was happening. I also discovered that for the first time in my life (despite many previous attempts) I was singing in the Spirit – because that's another thing I share with my father: lack of ability to dance and to sing!

A gross libel! It is true that in my first year of secondary school I twice got zero out of a hundred for singing. But I have sung in the Spirit, and in my early days it was as easy for me to dance in the Spirit as it was to speak in tongues – so I am dissociating myself from these comments! In the natural, yes, she takes after me. But – if I may reply with tongue in cheek – it has taken her a long time to come into the spiritual!

I heard myself singing in the Spirit. By this time I was very far out into the spiritual world, when Mary came over to me. At first I didn't know whether she was just encouraging me to continue moving out in dance, or what. But I turned my mind yet more Godward and began to move out into Him.

And then just suddenly something happened that was indescribable, but exquisitely beautiful. The verse that comes to mind is, ... *when I have put off this mortal flesh and have put on immortality*.[3] There was a sense of being absolutely unmade by God, physically as well as inwardly, as if becoming spirit instead of a creature encased in flesh and blood. I could not have done anything else but go down: there was no question about it. It was like going down in a wave of sweetness and of beauty.

There on the floor I found happening to me something that brought back a memory.

It had been another Monday night meeting about a year and a half earlier, when during the time of prayer I had suddenly become terribly conscious of God. For a moment it was like going into a thick, thick blackness. It was a lovely thing, not a bad but a good blackness. Beyond it, as if across a sea, I could see the glory of God and God in the midst of it, and knew that He was calling me out there. It was a new level of power, and I couldn't quite reach it, but I knew He was calling.

Afterwards I had read all the verses I could about God speaking to Moses out of the thick darkness. I noted too that Alison Speirs, who had suffered from years from migraine, also spoke of the velvet blackness as the hand of healing came on her.

And now I felt that thick darkness again.

I lay there very aware just of God. But at the same time there was something not quite completed, and I found one single cry going from me to God. Too private to reveal, it was a request that He would say one specific thing to me. Eventually I got myself on to my knees (totally surprised to find where I had been lying). I was still kneeling, still far out in God, when He sent His servant back, and the answer was given in the very words I had asked for, with unbelievable accuracy and precision. And something deep, deep down inside totally changed. There came a wealth of security and love, unbelievable love, in God.

That love had been a keynote of my life for years – ever since my first real, deep commitment to Christ when He absolutely flooded me again and again with the knowledge of His love. But now a verse began to live for me: *Henceforth I call you no more my servants, but my friends.*[4] Always connected in my mind with Abraham, it had seemed so out of reach. But I realized it was actually spoken to Christ's disciples, just before Gethsemane. And there is a sense of absolute oneness with God – I can't put it any clearer than that – in spite of sin that is part of human nature. One is totally merged into Him. And as the days have gone on I have realized just how deep and fundamental the change is. I remember my father speaking a number of years ago of finding how God had stood by him at an hour of deep need, under such fearful assault that he had almost died. (I knew how bad it had been because I had often seen him in that condition over the same period.) He had long known Christ and had faith for other people, but had always wondered what it would be like for him if he was really in desperation. But Christ had so come to him that there was born in him a new confidence in God, and he entered into a level of security that he hadn't known all these years. I knew as I listened that I wanted that, and I knew that if it had taken that length of time to happen to him, it hadn't happened to me. But I feel – I **know** it has happened now: a union that is indissoluble with God Himself. And I love Him: I cannot describe the love of God. Thinking of it afterwards, I realized that I was out there now in that sea: I had found that glory and that God.

One of the lovely things was the effect on our Tuesday night prayer meeting 24 hours later. The sense of God was overwhelming; some went down under it. One told me she had been hit by a bolt of light. Much of what I had received on the Monday night was transmitted to another in exquisite loveliness. She, without knowing anything of what had happened on the previous night, was overwhelmed with a sense of love.

The experience has left me with a deepened conviction that God can meet every need in every heart. This conviction had already seemed absolute; but now as specific lives have come before me the Spirit has highlighted a deeper level of need and given the absolute knowledge that God wants to meet it. At the very deepest, undiscovered levels of your being

He'll come in, He'll do it – oh, He'll do it for every one of us. The verse has lived for me as never before: *These things I have spoken unto you, that my joy might be in you.*[5] *I will be as the dew unto Israel* (Hosea 14:5). Praise His lovely Name.

Something that Grace said continued to echo in my mind. As she amplified it on another occasion:

I had thought that when God moves in revival the first thing that happens is conviction of sin that people may not even have known was there; things will be probed out. But there was nothing like that. There was instead the love of God.

For me also, even with my knowledge of revival, maybe partly **because of** my knowledge of revival, there had also been a kind of fear. I don't mean the fear of the Lord in a good sense, but just, 'How can we bear it?' And when God came to Grace He came in a total love. I found that He was doing that with many people. And even if what is lying down there is pretty grim and sordid, Christ will meet you with love. I now know that it is not always going to be according to my older idea of a big stick that would hit you. It is strange that we should get that notion, when we think of Scripture: how exceedingly gentle and kind He was to some of the worst of sinners.

One of many who received an overflow from Grace's experience was **Ruth**. A minister's daughter herself, with a canny Highland outlook, Ruth was sensitive to the presence of Christ. She was spiritually gifted and had charge of a young people's group in the Johnstone area. Despite her initial difficulty with the concept of asking for ministry of this strange new kind, she was increasingly drawn to the quality of experience that awaited those who yielded to the Spirit's draw:

I found it very hard at first to go forward when the new ministry began to flow in the church. One night there was a very deep incoming of God. It was very gentle, and there was a tremendous draw in it. When Mr Black made the appeal I didn't have the nerve at that point to respond. But as the time progressed I felt there was a real call and a desire to do so.

The first time I went forward I was very busy thinking, 'What will it feel like? At what point should I go down?' ... and this and that. Though I was very conscious of God and of His love, the newness of the experience was distracting me from going fully through. And I knew that I was to go forward again fairly soon after that, and that I was to forget all about the human side of things.

An opportunity came quite soon afterwards at the Sunday night youth meeting in Greenock, where God regularly met us in tremendous power. Grace was delayed, and she asked one or two of us to go ahead and start the meeting for her. As we began to pray with people, the same Spirit who had been in the earlier adult meeting fell on us in the after-meeting. One after another was going down as God came into the room.

Grace appeared on the scene, to my great pleasure – because deep down I really wanted to ask her if she would pray with me also. There came a point when she did that, and I had a very deep encounter with God. In the course of her prayer she said, 'The light of eternity has touched down upon you.' I wasn't conscious of all the externals, really – but I felt myself going out into a place of deep communion with God and a deep awareness of the light of eternity. A stillness of God built up in the room. At one point I opened my eyes briefly, to discover that everyone was either kneeling or prostrate before God. The whole room filled up with a heavy sense of the glory and the presence of God, mighty and powerful. And over my own being I felt wave upon wave upon wave of the light of eternity, and a sense of being brought before the reality of God and of eternal things, and of the call that was on my own life. It was very deep and very heavy and very still.

Towards the end of it, as I was seeing into spiritual places I was vividly aware of God's calling on the church and the kind of call He wanted to bring on certain lives. I became conscious of one in particular, and I felt from God's eternal perspective that the spirit of the evangel was on that life. And I felt revelation coming on myself, relative to that one. At the end I spoke to Grace, and it turned out that the person concerned had entered that night into a new dimension in that realm. It was very encouraging, because I knew that it really was revelation that God was giving.

There have been a number of times since then that I have gone forward. Some of the experiences are very private, and they have all been very precious to me. One of them I feel I can share.

We had a camp at Loch Lomond in March. In the Sunday morning meeting God came down on us in a really wonderful way. The depth of worship and revelation that was with us was quite awesome. I felt myself very deeply drawn into that meeting. One particular phrase had spoken to me when Grace had read from the Bible the words spoken of Christ relative to His baptism: 'The heavens opened upon Him.' There was an utter thrill inside me when she read those words, and they were with me all through the meeting. When I went home I spent most of the afternoon in my bedroom before God, and I felt that these words, 'The heavens opened upon Him,' were calling me in. I sensed there would be further ministry that night, and I was to go forward again. Though I hadn't spoken to anyone as far as I can recollect, when I went forward Grace prayed and said, 'The heavens are opening upon you,' and I felt again that light of eternity touch down upon me. I felt the sense of Christ and His baptism and His humbling before God, His purity, His cleanness, and the glory of that which came upon Him. And I found in my own being that something of that came down and has had a very deep impact on my life.

In Christ's own words,

> *This is life eternal, that they might know thee the only true God, and Jesus Christ, whom thou hast sent.*

The knowledge of God and His Christ that came through the new ministry was prized above all. The blessings of healing, deliverance and repentance described in some of the following chapters were an outflow of the presence of the Giver.

Notes

1. Grace Gault is in charge of our Greenock church. At the period to which this testimony belongs she had already occupied this position for several years. An impression of the breadth of her ministry can be derived from my book *War in Heaven and Earth* (New Wine Press, 1996), chapters 4, 6 and 7.
2. Mary Black's testimony appears in my *Christian Fundamentals* (New Dawn Books, 1991), chapter 4. She is also featured in *A View from the Floor* and *Further Views from the Floor*.
3. Paraphrasing 1 Corinthians 15:54.
4. See John 15:15.
5. See John 15:11.

Chapter 6

Healing in His Wings

Then shall thy light break forth as the morning, and thy healing shall spring forth speedily. (Isaiah 58:8)

Near the end of 1996 I asked for an impromptu report on a development which had pleased me very much. As readers of my other books will know, the miracle of healing had touched many lives in our company. But it became clear that we were now seeing an increase in this phenomenon.

A River of Healing

Introducing the subject, my daughter **Mary** referred to the promise that had come at the beginning of the year.[1]

Part of the New Year Word for 1996 was, *Thy health shall spring forth speedily*. Now though that word had lived for me, it was in a 'global' sense in that I felt it applied to the whole man, and I was open as to whether God would bring it to pass through the healing of inner wounds and hurts, psychological difficulties, or phobias, or through physical healing. Through the course of the year I have observed that many people have been released from phobias, and there has also been a great deal of emotional healing. Then just in the last week or two I became aware (almost accidentally, because it hadn't been particularly publicized) that quite a number of people had experienced physical healing also. There has been a quiet little river of healing, flowing in different parts of the movement. I felt that God should be given the glory for this.

As an illustration **Grace Gault** was asked to share what she had seen of the action of God in healing during 1996. Explaining that she would confine herself to healings she had seen firsthand, she first indicated the background. There had come to her an inner 'seeing' some weeks before the New Year Word was given:

It happened during our Sunday morning communion service in Greenock, during the worship time. I saw as it were in picture form the verse: *The sun of righteousness has arisen unto you with healing in his wings*. And the revelation was absolutely wonderful. I could see it. It was like a bird with its enormous wings outstretched, and pouring from these wings were rays and rays of light. They spoke of healing pouring down upon the earth and upon the church of Christ. In those rays there was inner healing, emotional healing, spiritual healing and deliverance, but there was also very definitely physical healing. As I spoke the words in prophecy, I was actually trembling with the power of what was being conveyed to my own spirit, and with the seeing I had in the spiritual world of these healing rays of the Lord Jesus Christ. They were pouring directly from Him. I felt that He would have me speak on that verse at New Year, and I did not speak about it until then. When Mary brought the New Year Word, the promise, *Thy healing shall spring forth speedily*, really lived for me. It tied up with the other verse, which has continued to

live. Just a few days ago there came over me again the
power of the glory of that revelation.

Grace's personal experience of the fulfilment of these
promises began with a healing of her own, which occurred
in February during the visit of Bruce Shimwell, one of the
associates of Elizabeth Austin:

> He described a condition almost word for word as I
> had described it to my husband that afternoon. He
> spoke of pain in the lower back coming down into the
> hips. I had recurring pain in my back, stemming, I
> think, from the time I had been nursing Miss Taylor,
> and aggravated by having a daughter whom I had to
> carry long after the age that most children are being
> carried. Physiotherapy had worked wonders, but the
> pain had returned and was so bad that I was again at
> the stage of rolling out of bed and taking a while to
> straighten. I had actually said to Wesley that after-
> noon, 'I think I'll need to go and see Elaine (the
> physiotherapist) again.'
> I did not respond to Mr Shimwell's appeal, think-
> ing, 'Well, it's not agony; there are people in a much
> worse condition.' But he prayed for me at the end of
> the meeting (not for healing: he didn't know anything
> about my condition), and as I was on the floor I felt
> something like a butterfly movement along what I
> know from my physiotherapist is the sacro-iliac joint.
> It was like muscles being undone. I had had no
> thought of healing until that point. I waited to be
> sure. And I have found that over the months my back
> has been all right. If ever a pain has come back it has
> just gone away again. I have risked carrying Christine
> again – and even she had got to the stage where she
> knew she wasn't to be carried.
> But beyond my own situation I discovered that a
> healing stream began to flow. It had sometimes
> happened before; but this time I felt it had come in a

way that was to stay. The next morning in our communion service in Greenock an older lady was healed of a throat condition. I had gone over to pray with her, but not for healing, and not knowing that the reason she had come to the service was because she hoped there might be ministry. Not long afterwards a nurse was healed of a sore leg and hip.[2] Then someone who had various pains throughout her body had a touch of healing one Sunday night in Greenock. A young woman who had been suffering for weeks from post-viral exhaustion and felt she couldn't go back to her work in that condition, was healed virtually instantaneously of the tiredness; an accompanying cough cleared itself in due course. Another condition for which she had recently had an operation, and which wasn't healing as it should, was also healed more or less instantaneously. When she went back to hospital the medical staff were very pleased with her condition. Last Sunday night in Greenock a mother who had been suffering from postnatal depression anxiety for about eighteen months since her second child was born, testified that she had been totally healed, and she is rejoicing in Christ.

Grace went on to sketch something of the inner side of the healing phenomenon:

I brought the matter before God, to see whether He really did want me to pray for people who were sick. I did not want to attempt what someone else might have done better, and risk destroying their faith: it's as simple as that. I felt God answer me very much as He had done regarding another ministry.

He said, 'Don't worry. If I want you to pray for somebody who's sick, I'll bring them to you.'

That very night Andrew Jewell, who had never asked me to pray with him for healing before, asked me to do so there and then![3]

I felt God say to me, 'Don't send him away. Isn't this exactly what I said to you?'

I have prayed with Andrew many times, and there has been wonderful revelation of Christ. But that night, so far as I know, he had a new revelation of the healing presence of the Christ who walked by Galilee: just as simple and as beautiful. And he was healed: praise God! He recognized that healing presence; and he recognized it later when he prayed for Gordon's healing.[4] And in our Sunday morning service not very long ago, aware of the healing presence, I was actually thinking of praying with Andrew without knowing that his back was in need of healing. Having discovered it shortly afterwards, I prayed with him during our young people's meeting for about one and a half minutes. Again that healing presence was unmistakable, and he was instantaneously healed. We both said to each other that it would have been harder not to believe that he was healed than it was to believe.

Grace then commented on the way in which the enemy assaults the healing ministry. A potent example was the case of Mike, whose healing is recorded in *A View from the Floor*. As she explained:

There is something very wonderful about what has happened to Mike. Influenced by the power that was generally flowing amongst us after the new ministry had come into our church, he had come forward, not for healing, but just for the ministry. The fire of God came right inside him, and he discovered that he was healed of a muscle condition that would eventually have consigned him to a wheelchair, in severe pain. In the early months of this year his wife told me one day in the bookshop that the pain had begun to come back. I was extremely distressed in my spirit, feeling that the glory of Christ was being assailed by Satan, and the power of the new ministry undermined. I felt terribly for Mike and Jean. I couldn't bear to think of Mike facing all that pain again – and he was not being at all offended in God over it; he was accepting it, he was being sweet about it; but the thought of the pain coming back just seemed to me unbearable, and that he might end up in a wheelchair – it was as if heaven had opened to him and was being snatched away. The verse kept coming to me, *An enemy hath done this* (Matthew 13:28). I really sought God, and I lifted a book about John G. Lake, a healing evangelist in the early decades of this century in America, asking God that He would speak to me from it. And it opened at a part where his own son had been healed of typhoid fever in an instant, but it had come back, and he had had to fight Satan over a period until that son was restored to health. I gave the book to Mike, feeling that God was saying we were to fight it. We prayed together, and his condition was stayed; but he wasn't healed until one night when he had come forward for ministry. Diana and I prayed with him and he met God very wonderfully. He has been totally well since – so well that he has taken a job, back into the working world! The glory is all God's.

I love the healing presence of Christ. There are many in our midst who are used in healing, and many others could tell also of healings that have happened. It is a wonderful aspect of Christ's ministry, and it is assailed. There has been some sickness amongst us, amongst some who are very deeply spiritual, and I think it is just part of the conflict before there is yet more of that healing glory of the Son of God – I think perhaps that's the most wonderful part of all, when the soul sees that revelation of the Lord Jesus Christ. Just shortly after Mike testified to his experience, a lady told me that the same thing had been happening to her. One Sunday night in the prayer meeting that Owen takes, she had gone into spiritual song and had been healed both in an inner sense and of an arthritic hip.[5] She now found that the arthritis was coming back, and hearing what had happened to Mike she asked for prayer. She was totally healed and, many months later, is still rejoicing in God.

In this report of Grace's I was particularly struck by Christ's promise that He would bring the sick to her. Questioned further, she said: 'That is the way it has happened every time, I think, since then. I have been quite amazed by it, feeling it has been God's doing that for some reason or other they have come.'

Meanwhile **Jennifer Jack**, the minister of our Falkirk church, had her own experience of the mantle of healing to relate:

Around the middle of the July camp week I felt that two words were highlighted for me. One was **healing** and the other was **deliverance**. I didn't know quite what God wanted to say about either of them, but in a very strange way it came about on the last night that Owen was one of the speakers, and healing was his theme.

At the end of that meeting there was a call for those seeking healing. I was one of many who responded. I was conscious of a mantle of healing falling upon myself and upon many others as they were receiving ministry. It was the mantle of the healing Christ. I have since discovered that within two to three weeks of that time in very different ways two of our own company in Falkirk were healed quite miraculously. One man's healing from a heart attack happened in the midst of a dream. As he wakened from the dream there was the sense of Christ speaking to him and of His healing power. (His healing has since been confirmed.) Within a few days of that, during our August camp a lady was healed of the effects of a heart attack. Listening to both of these testimonies at very different times, I was conscious of the same sense of the healing Christ and of His mantle.

I had been aware of that part of the New Year Word when it had been given months beforehand, and there had been times in between the New Year and the summer time when in the face of different needs I desperately prayed for that word to come into operation, but these things don't happen necessarily just because you are very keen that they should happen in a particular set of circumstances. And at the July camp it was as though Christ was saying to me, 'Look at what I am going to do. See how I am going to move.'

Just a few weeks ago one of our Falkirk people was healed in the Glasgow meeting of a chronic wrist condition. She had been told that she might have to give up her work as a secretary because the constant typing or word processing was aggravating the problem. She has now been six weeks or so totally without pain.

Another healing happened at the end of one of our meetings in Falkirk when the mother of a young family (with all of the pressure that that can bring) asked for prayer for constant tiredness and headache from which she had been suffering for weeks. A little later she told me that the headaches had gone instantly, and the tiredness had lifted completely within a day or two.

Like Grace, I have been conscious of the coming of Christ in that particular way – conscious of the fact that He said He would do it, the way in which He spoke to me about it, and the mantle of the Healer which I actually sensed had fallen upon those whom I heard tell of their healing.

Testimonies to Healing

One of those who furnished accounts of their own healing was **Andrew**, who testified to two of the incidents to which Grace had referred:

For as far back as I can remember I have had a problem with eating: not the problem that some people have – eating too much! – but that of not eating enough. Over the months leading up to the time that I went for prayer, I also began to be quite sick with it. I never discussed it with anyone, because the last thing you need is people fussing. But on a couple of occasions other people were present when the problem surfaced. Typically it would be in the middle of eating a meal, or afterwards, that all of a sudden it would come into my head that I wasn't going to be able to finish the meal, or was going to be sick. The minute that happened, it was as if I lost all control. On a few occasions I was actually physically sick. It got to the point where this had happened almost every time I had eaten during one particular week. Ultimately one evening, on the way home from a meal out, I had to stop the car in order to be sick. Frustrated, I thought, 'This is ridiculous. I'm going to speak to Mrs Gault about it and ask for prayer, because I cannot live like this any more.'

As we turned to pray, the sense of Christ that came was different from what I had felt before. Although I wouldn't say I knew immediately that everything was well, I knew that something had happened. Very soon it became clear that the sickness had passed away.

Since then there have been a couple of occasions where the same kind of symptoms began to appear but never again reached the previous level. I don't think there has been a single occasion since then when I have actually been physically sick, and there has always been a place of victory in Christ over it.

In September 1996 Andrew had already testified to the healing of his back:

Towards the end of a Saturday night meeting, when there's a time of ministry, very often Mr Black will ask me to help in catching people as they go down. On one such occasion I felt a sharp pain in the top of my right leg. Without thinking any more about it, I continued standing throughout the singing at the end of the meeting and felt no particular pain. It was when Mr Black closed in prayer and I went to sit on the bench at the side that the pain went up the right side of my back. I felt my head pulled down towards my right shoulder, and my shoulder somehow pulled up. Neither sitting nor bending could I find a comfortable position. I went home to bed, and when I woke up on Sunday morning the pain was not only in the right side of my back but also in the left, and right up my back on either side of my spine. I could not sit in any position or even stand for any length of time without it becoming really sore.

After the Sunday morning meeting in Greenock I mentioned it briefly in passing to Mrs Gault. Back home, I spent Sunday afternoon in a hot bath – because that was the only way to get a bit of relief from the pain.

After the meeting that night Mrs Gault, who was sitting beside me, said, 'Andrew, how's your back?'

I said, 'It's still quite sore.'

She said, 'Would you like me to pray with you?'

I said, 'Yes, please!'

She put her hand on my back and said, 'Now just go to Christ as if He was standing there as He used to do on the shores of Galilee, when you read that they brought the sick to Him and He healed all of them.'

And suddenly it became more than words that she was saying. I could actually feel that it was happening. It would have been harder for me to hold on to the pain than just to look upwards to Christ and let it go. I went through to God, and we closed in prayer. There was no pain at all in my back, and I turned to Mrs Gault and said, 'Hey, Mrs Gault, it feels OK!'

On my way out, I was bending and stretching and pressing it and so on. I was going up to stay with a friend who had just moved into college halls of residence, and I would have to spend the night on his floor. Previously I had been thinking, 'There's no way I'll be able to do this if my back's like this, because it's agony.' But I went up, my back was fine, and all week there has been no pain at all. Praise God!

Ironically, it is possible that some of Andrew's audience had noticed him hobbling up to the platform to give this testimony to the healing of his back! His limp, he assured us, was the result of a recent football injury. He told us a few months later how God healed him yet again:

'No more football for you till the end of January!'

This was the specialist's ultimatum on the pain in my knees that had been bothering me throughout 1996, especially towards the end of the year. There was no doubt that the pain in my knees had been aggravated when I started playing football once a fortnight as part of a church outreach; I had also been asked to play for my college football team on a couple of occasions. The point came when instead of jumping upstairs two or three at a time I could only manage one at a time. More than a few stairs always found me in considerable pain by the time I got to the top. Sometimes my left knee in particular was on the verge of collapse.

It was around the end of November that I eventually saw the specialist. He conducted a series of tests – felt my knees, did X-rays and all the rest of it – and informed me that I had something called *condramalasiapatella*. Directing me to the physiotherapist, he said, 'If it is not any better when you come back in January, we'll do a spot of keyhole surgery on that left knee.'

But before January dawned, God intervened.

Throughout our last Saturday night meeting of 1996 I felt the presence of God on me in quite an unusual way, with a physical tingling sensation all over. When Mr Black gave the call for ministry I went forward, and as he prayed with me I went prostrate.

Meanwhile, in the course of leading worship, Miss [Mary] Black spoke these words: 'Let him that readeth the vision run with it.'[6] As soon as she said that, I felt the tingling going right through my body, and those words stayed vividly with me: **Let him that readeth the vision run with it.**

Although it crossed my mind that God had possibly touched my knees, I did not really think any more about it until the following Wednesday night when I had to stay overnight in a flat up four flights of stairs. This of all places was normally the one where I really noticed the pain in my knee. But that night I ran right up the stairs and was at the top before it suddenly hit me: 'Wait a minute – I did not have a single twinge of pain there.' I started wondering, 'Maybe that really was God . . .'

Then three days later, while painting a room at The Cedars in Greenock, we needed something from the attic. Now for most houses the attic is up one flight of stairs or so, but at The Cedars you need to go up three or four flights!

'Right, here we go – two at a time and I'll see how quickly I can get to the top.' And up I went into the attic, without any thought of pain at all!

Also, my knee used to make a really loud click every time I bent it. One night sitting in halls with the other students I said, 'You know, I have a really sore knee. Listen to this.' When I clicked it, they all said, 'Wow!' Now that has disappeared too.

I do feel that God has had a hand in this and that He has really touched me. It is surely part of the fulfilment of last year's New Year Word, that our healing would spring forth speedily.

✤ ✤ ✤

In the middle of 1996 Andrew himself had been used in the ministry of healing for the first time in his experience. Seeking ministry on this occasion was **Gordon**, a member of our Falkirk congregation; appropriately, it was for a football-related injury! The news of his healing was initially brought to us by Jennifer:

> Around the end of March, during a game of football, Gordon cracked heads against another football player with such force that it was heard, I understand, at the other end of the football pitch. He continued to play until the end of the game, but there were already ominous signs – for example, he kept asking every few seconds what the score was – and it was obvious that things were not too well inside his head!
>
> Within the next few days he went to the doctor and was taken to hospital for X-ray. Since no damage was shown up, it was thought that he had a simple case of concussion, which was expected to pass off within two or three days.
>
> Back at work, he continued to experience very severe headaches and forgetfulness. He was taken on his boss's instructions to hospital in Edinburgh, where again various tests and scans showed nothing wrong. This was a great relief, obviously, but it didn't solve the problem.
>
> Such was his inability to think in front of a computer screen that he had to take five weeks off work.
>
> The end of March was the very worst time for him to go off. It was just before the end of the financial year – his bosses had banned him from playing football again at the end of the financial year, and I

think his wife has banned him from playing football ever, no matter what time of year! But the problem continued through many weeks.

I remember he spoke to me on one or two occasions about the thought of seeking for healing. But Gordon is one of these people who likes to think things through carefully before he takes any action. When he takes action it's usually definite and long lasting, but he doesn't get there overnight. He didn't feel that just because he was unwell he should automatically seek healing. After prayer was made for him (unasked) one night in Falkirk, he felt an improvement, and he was becoming more open to God moving in that way. And then just a couple of weeks ago he told me he was coming to the point where he felt it would be right to seek for healing, probably on Saturday night. He felt he would be prepared by that time.

Others can fill in what happened next. I do know that since that time he has had no headaches whatsoever.

As it happened, that Saturday night was the first occasion that I had encouraged Andrew to be more than a 'catcher' and actually to lay hands on. He told the story from his own perspective:

Some time before Gordon's healing, while reading a book about someone who was used very much in that way, I felt God speaking to me. Also, the verse that we were given in the New Year Word really lived: *Your healing will spring forth speedily*. Not knowing whether it was right to look for God moving in that way or not, I left it very much with Him, saying, 'Lord, I'd love to see You move in that way, but I'm not going to do anything about it, and I'm not going to speak to people about it. I'm just going to leave it with You and see what happens.' I think I spoke to just one other person about it.

A few weeks, maybe a couple of months, passed. I had really forgotten about it on the night that Mr Black asked me to minister.

I went over to Gordon and he said, 'Andrew, actually I've come for healing.'

I said, 'Right, we'll just pray.'

To the best of my memory, I hadn't prayed for anyone's healing before. But I thought, 'I'm not going to pray, "If it's Your will . . ." I'm just going to go for it, and this will show me if it really was God who was speaking to me, or if I'm just making it up in my head.'

As I prayed I felt the anointing of God physically on me. The words that came were, *The burning touch of Christ is on you, Gordon.* It felt indeed like the burning, healing touch of Christ, and Gordon went down. And that was all.

At the end of the meeting I looked over to see if there was any difference, and saw Gordon holding his head.

'Oh, well, that's it,' I thought. 'OK, God, you've shown me.'

I didn't really think any more about it until later when Gordon came and said that he hadn't had any more headaches. And I hadn't known any of the background until Miss Jack gave it just now.

Gordon's own account, given four months later, illustrates both the seriousness of his condition and the spiritual journey that underlay his eventual healing:

The headaches that had been coming on during the day of the accident drove me out of the adult meeting and into the kids' meeting, which was being taken by Alison Speirs.[7] Her message that night was about a little boy who banged his head! But it wasn't a nice little story: it was quite a heavy story, about how the sins of your youth affect you into adulthood. I knew

73

(if it was for me) what it was about, but decided not completely to agree with the speaker!

Back at work, along with the headaches I began getting memory loss. This went on for a period of three months. One or two stories will show what it was like. One day before being put off work I went to the drinks machine and dropped my money in for a coffee. Then, apparently forgetting that I had already paid, I deposited more coins and got another coffee, which I plunked on top of the one below! You sit there looking at it and just can't believe it, because it seems so strange to have done such a thing. On another occasion I phoned someone twice within 10 minutes to arrange for a lift in his car. For weeks I was oblivious to this, since he very nicely refrained from comment there and then.

By the time I went to the doctor the situation was serious. I didn't know my name or who I was, and I couldn't subtract 7 from 100. The doctor didn't believe I was an accountant. I was quite pleased that it was my dad who was with me; the situation was not something one would want people in general to know!

Mr Black offered me prayer a few days after this, when the memory loss intensified. But in my wisdom I decided this was not a good idea. The neuro-surgeon had said I should be OK in two or three weeks, and I opted to believe the neuro-surgeon and not Mr Black. But I also think that at that time I didn't have faith for healing, and that God wanted to do a deeper work in me, connected with what had been said in the kids' meeting.

During those three months I had not been back at the Saturday night meeting until one occasion when someone was testifying to how she had found spiritual healing, and following the spiritual healing had come physical healing.[8] That night reminded me very much of my previous visit, bringing home to me what the problem was and my need for ministry. The reason for my reluctance was that when I first came into the church I had looked for deliverance on the subject and hadn't found it. God had graciously allowed me to continue for a period of time, finding Him in different ways but knowing that He did want this sorted out. So I didn't go lightly for ministry. When the time came, I didn't just want to go down under the power of the Spirit; I wanted to tell someone my reason for coming. That wasn't easy to do. But it was made easy – this is where God knows us and knows our needs so well. At the front, Mr Cleary approached me.[9] Other people receiving ministry up to that point had gone down under the power as hands were laid on, but he actually took me aside and sat me down to talk to me. I felt so comforted by the fact that the servant of God seemed to know my needs and knew that I wanted to talk. He spoke to me for a bit, and laid on hands. The moving of God on me wasn't really pleasant, to be honest – but what He was dealing with wasn't pleasant either. Yet I knew straight away it had been sorted out, after having troubled me for many, many years.

Over the next week the head problems continued; I'd gone back to work but was getting headaches all day for sustained periods. Several times that week I wanted to cry at work – not a manly sort of thing to do, but I wasn't coping. At church in Falkirk I couldn't sing because of the headaches. I really enjoy moving out in that way and felt that I wasn't getting a channel into God.

I came forward the next Saturday night – just because the word had been spoken the week before, 'The physical healing will come after the spiritual healing,' and I knew I had been spiritually healed. I didn't feel good in the service; I didn't have an anointing; I hadn't 'got through', so to speak: I hadn't found a deep place in God. But the word had been spoken, so I came forward that night, and it was

Andrew who prayed for me. I remember being very aware when he laid on hands that this servant of God was anointed. The minute he touched me I just about fell over and actually stopped myself because I got such a fright – and really then had to go out into God for the ministry to proceed. Since then I've had two headaches ... normal ones! The headaches associated with my injury stopped completely from that point on. I give God the glory for that.

The next healing to be related here brought great joy both to the one concerned and to those who had seen her suffering. One of those listening to Grace's report of Christ's healing ministry was **Karen**, a Post Office employee. Nearly three months later she told us what had happened then:

About three years ago I started to experience quite a lot of pain on the right side of my back. I didn't understand what it was, since I hadn't fallen or done anything to cause it. Eventually it got so bad that I had to see the doctor. Tests revealed that I had only one kidney. The right side was the one without a kidney, and the doctors thought that this was the cause of the problem.

The pain continued and became very debilitating. For eighteen months I very rarely had a night's sleep and never had a day without pain. It affected every area of my life, spiritually as well as physically. Unable to bend down without pain, I was like an old woman getting up. I couldn't lift anything heavy and had very little mobility.

A radioactive scan at the Southern General showed that the problem was muscle spasms in my back. When I returned for a check-up a month later, the doctor told me that the condition was not only incurable but would progressively worsen, and that I must adapt my life around it. Meanwhile the pain, which was excruciating, had started to go down my legs and down my arms. Sometimes it was very dark, very black, with the pain. Even though I knew that people round me were caring for me, loving me, praying for me, being with me and bearing me up, there were still times that I felt cut off and isolated. Through it all, I knew that Christ was near, and He was faithful. There was never a day that He was not there; there was never a time that He left me. There is a verse which I like to paraphrase: *In my weakness he will be my strength.* I found not only the head knowledge but the reality, the day-to-day living of that verse as I got up in the morning, that He was my strength. It got to the stage where I thought I would have to cut down my work to part time or else give it up completely. Through all, I knew that Christ could heal: that if it was His will He could just breathe the words that heal and I would be whole again. But I also knew that His desire is different for every one, and if He desired to heal me, then that was His will, but if He didn't, then it was His will also.

On 30 November I came forward for healing. It was the night that Mrs Gault spoke here on the new depth of ministry in healing that Christ was bringing her into, and how she felt that God was going to bring more healing into the church. Although I did not doubt that God could heal, I knew as she was speaking that her words were like water to feed the faith in me, to let it grow. The sensation is hard to describe. It was like a joy, but it was a hush inside, an inner expectation that I'd never felt before although I knew that He could heal. I didn't allow myself to go right out into it, because I didn't know whether it was to be that night. But I went forward anyway. I remember standing there, praying, 'Lord, if it is Your will, praise Your Name. But if it isn't, then praise Your Name.

And if I bear it till eternity, You will be my strength.'
It wasn't a false commitment. I really meant it –
because I was living it anyway up until that point.

Mrs Gault prayed with me. I'll never forget the
words she said as I went down: 'Lord, we feel
the faith of your child increase.' As she said that, the
overwhelming joy of Christ's presence came over me –
because it was vital to me that Christ should know
that I knew He could heal. It was a pain of desire that
He know, because I believed He could. And as she
said that, I was lost in Christ – I went right out
into Christ and into worship. I was so aware of Him
I lost consciousness of myself and of all around. I
couldn't say that I felt a healing presence; I just
knew I was lost in worship. It was wonderful. It was
as if for a moment I had come out of myself and
gone into that land that knew no pain, and it was
wonderful.

I came back – ! There was a returning awareness of
my surroundings, and of the fact that I was still in
pain, but it didn't touch me. Lying there I wondered,
'How am I going to get up – with dignity?' But I got
up anyway and went back to my seat and didn't allow
myself to think, 'Am I healed or am I not?' I just let
it be.

It wasn't till a week later that Karen realized that a
miracle had taken place.

While at work I bent down and picked up a really
heavy bag – and I thought, 'Wait a minute! I didn't
feel any pain.' I got up and thought, 'I can't do that!'
Then I realized, 'I just did it!'

The joy of it is absolutely amazing. But I kept the
miracle to myself, because I wanted to be sure that it
had happened. Whereas I had been attending the
physiotherapists at the pain clinic and had worn a
Tens machine constantly, for the last two-and-a-half

months (I don't know the exact date, because I didn't realize it till a week later) I haven't used my Tens machine or had any painkillers at all, nor have I had a sleepless night through pain. I ran up the stairs on Friday night past and got to the top, and it was as if God just stopped me in my tracks and said, 'Right, Karen, it's time to tell.' I just praise God. There are no words. I can't say anything! Gratitude seems so small. Overwhelming joy ... it's indescribable to know that not only can I stand for a song and lift one of my hands, but I can stand through the whole of the worship time, and lift both hands at once. I am free to worship God in body as well as in spirit. I praise His holy Name that He is eternally faithful, and all glory goes to Him.

We may imagine what it meant to one who had been in intense pain, declared 'incurable', suddenly to meet the living Lord, who has never heard that word. Oh, for a surging faith to touch His church, to enter into the realm where miracle actually happens.

Healing Rays

During the week that followed the report on manifold healing, I myself took a chill. It started one particularly cold night with a tickle in the throat. It would not be ignored, and when I had scarcely eaten for three days I realized it was serious! Thinking I had better get some penicillin, I called the doctor.

Such was my physical condition that I found myself very uncertain about attending the next Saturday night meeting. I had not missed one through illness since they began. Even when my ankle was badly fractured in a fall, God provided. As I pondered, my mind went on to some scripture for a possible sermon, but it seemed like a dead end. I was not going to force anything; if it was the first Saturday I wouldn't be there, then so be it.

Suddenly I felt God speak to me. Some visitors arrived just at that point, and the full message didn't come until I settled down again. And then I had a very lovely experience. It was as though I was in the healing rays of His presence for a time. Now I don't mean that there was a dramatic miracle; but there was the feeling of the warmth and the healing of God. The theme that came for the meeting, though not connected in my mind with my own situation, was nevertheless appropriate: 'My times are in Thy hand.'

It was not until afterwards that someone pointed out the juxtaposition of events: the public giving of glory to God for His healing presence, and my own illness almost immediately afterwards. If this was some kind of response from the enemy, God's was the victory.[10]

Notes

1. From the experience of many years we had come to expect a scriptural 'word' or 'promise' from God when we met for our New Year conference. The promise given in 1996 was from Isaiah 58:8, 11 and 12.

2. This healing included an unusual and very lovely element. The nurse concerned was Linda J (see chapter 3), and the pain felt to her like phlebitis. After prayer one Saturday night the pain receded but worsened again until in the early hours of Monday morning, after turning to God for help, she had a dream in which Grace prayed for her again. There was a phenomenal presence of the Spirit, and the actual physical healing was accompanied by a lingering sense of God throughout the rest of the day.

3. See below in this chapter. Andrew's earlier experience of the new ministry is recounted in *A View from the Floor*, chapter 6.

4. See below in this chapter.

5. The reference is to Owen Martin, whose testimony is in chapter 8.

6. The allusion is to Habakkuk 2:2.

7. For Alison Speirs, see chapter 1 and note 2 *ibid*.

8. This was 'Sue F', whose testimony to an earlier experience under the new ministry is in chapter 10.

9. Robert Cleary, a founder-member of the Struthers movement, is in charge of our Gourock church. See chapter 10.

10. This episode has been included at the request of my daughter, who is co-author of the book.

Chapter 7

Driving Deeper

By mid-1995 a number of us felt that in the early days of the new ministry at times there had been quite phenomenal power, but that more recently there had come a kind of levelling out. While many were still receiving ministry, we were not sure that the work was deepening. I began to question in my own heart whether we were really getting all that God had for us, and going into the deeps that He wanted us to enter. We are peculiarly made, and it is very easy for us to grow casual and cool. It is also true that when you are lying down there on the floor and God is dealing with you personally, nobody but yourself and God knows exactly what is happening. It may be that decisions made were not always kept, which had they been made in a more open way would have been more difficult to break. Be that as it may, there came a feeling in me for driving deeper. I believed, without claiming prophetic insight on the matter, that that first glorious wave with the manifestation of the love of God, His tenderness, His gentleness and His forgiveness, would be followed by another and deeper wave.

At the July camp of 1995 there were one or two signs of what I was looking for. The case of **Alistair** shows how God had gone down into the depths and was changing people at those depths. This is what revival is, and this is what Christ came to do. Alistair's later account of his experience was punctuated by appreciative laughter from his audience. With an academic training in philosophy and politics and a developing career as a lecturer in information science, he had to learn how to subject his own thinking to the mind of Christ.

This might sound a bit incoherent, but I really don't mind so long as the glory goes to Christ for what He has done for me. I'm just going to 'tell it like it was', and is.

I think it goes back to dryness in my spirit over months if not years, and also the issue of the mind, and associated with that the acceptance of authority. There had been a number of matters where I had not really agreed with the way the church (Mr Black in particular) had handled things, and this brought me into conflict with church authority. I could make a big case for what I believed, but it would still be wrong.

The new dispensation of ministry was part of the problem, because my mind was not quite in step with it. To the natural man it's just plain silly, isn't it – lying on your back with your hands in the air, singing! – or laughing your head off when no one has cracked a joke!

I hadn't been 'anti-', but I had been sceptical, though I had gone forward once or twice. On the second occasion at least I had had a blessing, but not a deepening. It had passed.

So the mind was, I suppose, in revolt to some extent against this new ministry. And I had wondered what my place was in this phase the church was going into, because it's so different from when I came into it fifteen years ago. The goalposts have moved in various ways. We have developed new forms of expression – but I wondered what was my niche in it. My mind had said (and the stakes were quite high), 'Would you not be happier in a different kind of church? A more 'normal' evangelical church with an emphasis on systematic Bible studies and this kind of thing that the mind likes?'

It was at this juncture that Elizabeth Austin, signally used in the ministry of the word of knowledge, visited our Glasgow church. Alistair continues:

> I was hoping for something really nice from her, because I had been praying about the situation and had actually put things right with Mary the previous Monday. In the course of a long and entirely satisfactory chat with her, she had answered a lot of questions I had had. I really had put the past behind me.

To Alistair's way of thinking all had been sorted out, and he could progress from there. But God in His mercy sees deeper than we see, and He had in mind something far better for His child than that he should continue on more or less the same level as before. To pierce through to the deeper level that He wanted, the surgeon's knife was necessary – and it hurt.

To his dismay, the words addressed to him through God's servant were not what he had hoped for:

> She singled me out, and it was a rebuke – there is no way around that. She said that I had done some things my own way (a point with which I could not easily argue). I know how Ananias felt now (well, not quite)! It cut me to the quick, of course – even though some 'nice' things were said as well. It's like the sky falls in on you, and I was wounded.

The church camp started almost immediately after this eventful occasion. Alistair could not attend all of it but was fortunately able to be present for the whole of the Wednesday, on which as it happened an extra 'tarry' meeting had been arranged.[1] It was to prove a fateful and wonderful day.

Several people prayed with Alistair as he broke through into a new dimension:

> Ruth Gollan came to pray with me first, which she has done over the years every now and again. I have always had a really clear and encouraging word from her. She laid hands on me and said, 'Coming under the authority of Christ' – and it was just exactly right. She also said, 'Go out to Christ.' I am quite a reserved person, but I knew what she meant, because this new ministry, this new dispensation, is about going out to Christ (isn't it?) without reserve.
>
> Then one or two others including Grace and Diana came over and laid hands on me. The Spirit came very powerfully on me. The same theme came through their ministry, and I moved into tongues very, very deeply. I am so thankful that they persevered and didn't disappear as soon as I started speaking in tongues. Diana said, 'Go deeper, go deeper, go deeper' – even when the meeting had ended, and I was beginning to feel a bit embarrassed and self-conscious, because of course everyone would be looking at me. But I passed that, and Diana was adamant that I had to go through into a deeper place.
>
> We went through for quite a long time, and then there was a sort of pain barrier. Now this isn't pain from childhood trauma; I think this was – if I can sound like a philosopher for a second – the **angst** at the centre of our beings. That's where God reached: the pain at the centre of the being, the pain of being cut off from God from birth. God went there, and I went through that into a place of peace beyond that, and fantastic liberty. As I obeyed the injunction (again) to 'go out to Christ,' I found I was going into movement, at least with my hands, and that for me is a miracle! I'd always admired people who stand up and do it, and thought, 'How wonderful that you've got the guts to do that.' But here I was

doing it! And possibly people were seeing it, and I didn't care! I was past that, and I was through to Christ.

Sometimes one has an experience at camp of a wonderful blessing, and then it dissipates when one leaves – not necessarily wrongly, but the feeling, the 'feel-good' factor, fades as one moves on. But it hasn't happened this time. God has taken new ground in me. He has reached into a much deeper place near the centre of my being, and I **am** in a new place. It has been a major experience for me, and I am with God. The dryness has gone; I feel the rains of the Holy Spirit. I feel I am closer to God, and it has just been wonderful. God has compensated for that blow He dealt me – which was deserved – and has taken me into what has been happening in the church in the past few months. I feel I am right in the swim of the new movement now. I thank Him for all He has done: for His mercy, His forbearance, and His perseverance.

Many of us had really felt for Alistair on the earlier occasion. Elizabeth Austin is a very gentle and kind person, but she is also very firm. A mouthpiece of God has no choice. If you are given a word from God, you dare not alter that. On the surface it may seem quite incorrect; it may not even seem true to the speaker. But there is the knowledge that it is the word of God. God knows things in us all, and His judgment is often very different from ours or that of our friends about us. The assessment of God can be a very terrible thing, but it is also wonderful and glorious, and you see the fruit that it has brought.[2]

I liked what Alistair said about God going down into that inmost part of being, for this was exactly what I was looking for. It is a going into that part that has never been touched before, in many cases. There is an emancipation into an abundant life for us every one: He came that we might have life and that we might have it abundantly (John 10:10). Some Christians enjoy a measure – but that upsurging, powerful life of God, with the joy and the wellbeing that there is in Christ! To get there you have to break through that last deep part, that it may be filled up with the life of God.

Listening to Alistair testify was **Graham**, a risk management expert, who had had an experience in some ways quite different but in others remarkably similar. He was clearly moved throughout the sharing of his own testimony:

> I rejoice with you, Alistair – your face shone when you gave testimony, and it's lovely to see what God can do to a life. God has changed me too: absolutely tremendous, right to the very core of my being, incredible.
>
> Where do I start? That's the end of the story!
>
> A number of years ago I got caught up in a traumatic situation. Though not a direct player, I was certainly conscious of things going on. Without being particularly aware of a spiritual dimension, I got entangled in it. Things moved on and settled. I even said, 'Sorry,' to certain people; I put my back into this church; I gave all I had, and I was determined this was where my place of worship was to be. I wanted God; God knew that. I loved Him; He knew that too. I gave all I had to Him, as far as I could go. People have prayed with me over a number of years; I couldn't give any more. I knew God loved me, and I knew I loved Him. But that seemed to be as far as I could go.
>
> On Thursday night Diana spoke very pointedly about the awesomeness of God, a subject that is very close to my heart too. I felt to stand (which was unusual for me) and, when the opportunity was given, to go forward for prayer.
>
> As we walked down to the hall for ministry, I said, 'Lord, You know my heart. If there is anything that I haven't done to make myself repent, please sort it

now.' I was absolutely determined to find that way through. I didn't know where I was going; I just wanted to know a deeper place in God. You know that you get to that point where you are on a plateau, and you've got to punch your way through.

When we were divided up for ministry, Grace prayed with me. She and I had talked before about this legacy, so to speak, being touched in me. We entered into prayer in tongues. In my mind's eye – and I'm not a 'picture' person at all – I seemed to see barriers like curtains, and I was being encouraged to walk into the arms of Christ, just as if He had His arms outstretched for me to run into Him. It felt like going through curtains, closer and closer to Him.

The prayer time finished. Now I don't understand all this. But something had happened. Not something you could touch or feel, not something that you could put your finger on in recollection, or anything like that – but something deep in the kernel of my being had been touched. And I knew it had been touched, and I was happy!

I went back into the meeting praising God. When I woke up in the morning, my mind turned to God – and He was still there. The new horizon was still there – it looked lovely. In the meeting, God came down again, and I felt I could go into that same place. In the afternoon while we were in and around the caravan, I was conscious of God being there and also of the bliss of going about ordinary things, feeling a different presence of God from what I had ever felt before in my daily walk. I also felt a churning in myself, just before the meeting. I hadn't done anything to cause a dampening of my spirit, but I just felt I wanted to push that bit further in towards Him to make sure He was still there. And He was!

I couldn't describe to you the sensation with which I ran up to the tent to check that the children were OK, all the while exclaiming, 'Yes!'

I rejoice that God is touching right down in the inner kernel of our hearts. Some of us have tried for a long time and have done the best we can, and we can't do any more. God has got to touch you – and it is in His time. The understanding now of the spiritual dimension is greater than I've ever known before. I hadn't done anything particularly wrong; I had cleared all that. There was no spirit of evil or anything in me. It was almost as if the spirit of evil was outside of me, preventing me from going any further. It wasn't my fault. I know that. But God did it, and I glorify His Name. I look forward to one chapter closing and another chapter opening, to see what God can do.

That, if you knew the innerness of it, is a very remarkable testimony, and one from which we can learn a great deal. There are times when we can have our mind cleared in so far as we know, but still be subconsciously influenced by things that have happened. Pushed down and perchance never solved, they hang there like a curtain. And the devil can use such circumstances to prevent a soul getting right through to God. What has happened is a clearing of things that have been barriers and problems, held not consciously but down in the subconscious. It is into this deep subconscious realm that the Holy Spirit is now moving in many lives. When people are touched at that level they can go into the glory and know what it is to have fullness of life in Christ. It seems as though God is not willing to leave any debris in any of our lives. Again and again people say, 'He has gone right down...' He clears out things that they didn't even know were there until He began to act.

If Graham's barrier represented itself to him as a veil or curtain, **Ronnie** felt that his was an impenetrable wall. Unlike Graham and Alistair, he had a very good idea of what the problem was. Comparatively young in his Christian walk, he was aware of a deep hardness within.

'That's me she's speaking about,' he thought, as he sat in the same meeting as Graham, listening to Diana's call to holiness.

I felt unlovely just sitting there. Something within me was not right with God: I could feel it, and knew what the problem was. Within me there was a hardness, but because of circumstances in the past I just kept putting it down into the back of my mind. Something had to be done, because I couldn't live with myself. I was going round in circles, unable to get through to Christ at all. If only God would touch me without any effort from me ... but it wasn't happening.

So at the invitation to come forward, I thought, 'I need to get this dealt with, to get it up and out.'

On the way for ministry, I felt an inner shaking; I know now it was the Holy Spirit moving upon me. While waiting for prayer, I started sobbing uncontrollably like a big child – something that had never happened before. God was already preparing me.

When Pauline approached me, I didn't know where to start or what to ask.

I simply said, 'It's as if I'm going round in circles. There is a deep hardness in my heart, and I can't get through to Christ.' No matter how much I tried in meetings, tried to go out in tongues, pray, I just couldn't get anywhere. It was as if I was hitting a brick wall.

Pauline and I prayed in tongues. I was getting through to some extent, but the wall was still there. There was a part deep within that was holding back, a deep, inner root that I couldn't get to – and didn't want to get to. Pauline said, 'You need to go through. It's like a brick wall, and it's as if you're doing karate. In karate the object is to go through.'

Meanwhile, having noticed Ronnie trembling and crying earlier as he sat waiting for ministry, I returned for reasons of my own to observe the outcome.

We turned to prayer again, and Mr Black said, 'There's a lot moving and coming up. You're getting through so far, but not far enough. You need to hit the root, you need to go through.'

I was totally exhausted! But I kept going. As Pauline resumed praying with me, I said, 'Lord, You'll need to take me through, because I can't do it on my own.'

Then I started going forward ... and forward ... and by God's grace I got through!

Up until then, no matter how many meetings I came to, no matter how much I praised God, I couldn't get there. But God took me there. He has changed a part within me: He has touched the inner hardness. It is an ongoing process, but already there is a newness, a light, and a peace, and I have felt God's love. As Pauline said, 'God's love and God's forgiveness are with you.' In spite of the hardness He had to deal with, God accepted me. Praise His Name.

Watching Ronnie receiving ministry, I was reminded of an occasion when Miss Taylor and I had seen a man receive tremendous deliverance. About fourteen or fifteen demons had come out: she could see and identify them.

'That's wonderful,' I thought. 'I'll go home very happy.'

But not Miss Taylor.

'No,' she said, 'the oldest and the worst of them is still there. It is very deep down in the personality and thinks it is hidden, but I can see it, and it will have to come out. It will come up from the roots and out through the mouth.' That was that – and, sure enough, it was true.

There seems to come that clear knowledge that while much has happened, the vital bit, the full deliverance, has not yet come. There is a humorous side to this, even in the midst of terribly serious things. Here in Ronnie's case is a man being told, 'Just imagine it's a brick wall. You go full tilt and bash right through that wall!' Ronnie leapt, and Christ caught him. At the very moment he leapt at the wall and drove through it he was delivered. There is something worth knowing. It can take that degree of determination and application for the wall to break, and you'll not get hurt, and the demon power will be broken. Where there is a need deep down, God goes to the very depths.

✢ ✢ ✢

Very different from Ronnie's is the story told by **Carolyn**, but it too illustrates the power of God to deliver from deeply entrenched attitudes or mindsets and to take the individual into a spiritual realm far beyond their own power to enter.

It was only a few months since Carolyn, a student in physiotherapy, had begun attending our services and received her baptism in the Spirit. The denomination to which she belonged was not sympathetic to Pentecost, and eventually she was faced with a critical decision:

At Easter God blessed me very much, and He spoke to me about leaving the church I was in. It was a very difficult decision to make. It hurt my family, and it was not easy explaining to the elders what God had asked me to do, because as far as they were concerned I wasn't obeying Him by going to a pentecostal church. I think they thought I was a bit out of my mind, speaking in tongues and the rest of it! But I did move, and a few weeks ago I came full time into the Struthers church in Greenock. And I thought, 'Well, this hasn't been too bad. My mum's been really supportive, and not once have my parents tried to stop me.'

So the 'physical' move hasn't been too difficult. But a few Sunday nights ago at the young people's prayer meeting in Greenock, when Mrs Gault came over and prayed with me, I started crying and crying. I couldn't get through to God, and the pain of it was really hurting. I couldn't understand what the problem was.

As far as I was concerned I had made that commitment: I was in the church.

It was only when speaking to Mrs Gault afterwards that I realized the need to make a deeper spiritual commitment to what God has called me to. The physical side of making a change was easy. But for the past few weeks there had been crazy doubts in my mind. The devil was attacking my mind something awful. I am quite an introspective thinker anyway, and a lot of the fears and doubts that had gone when I received my baptism were coming back again. Stupid though they were, they were stopping me from getting through to God. I couldn't fight them, and it was making me miserable. But there was a determination I was going to stand to my calling. God had called me into this church, even though it was not what I had been brought up with. Throughout last week at camp, throughout the meetings, the prayer time and the worship time, it took all my energy just to stand firm. It was getting me down, because I thought, 'Is this ever going to end?' My greatest desire was to be able to meet God and get through into His presence.

On Thursday night during the singing at the beginning Miss (Mary) Black came over and prayed with me. Quite soon after the Easter conference I had started going into movement and dance in the Spirit. At first when I heard that this sort of thing went on I was quite reserved about it, because I had never heard of it before. Dancing in the Spirit – what on earth is this? But God led me into it. Initially I found it quite difficult to know when the anointing was there, but after receiving prayer I was able to go into dance in the Spirit more and more. During the camps I hadn't been doing so; it was taking all my energy just to concentrate on the fact that God was still on the throne no matter how I was feeling or what thoughts were in my mind.

When Miss Black prayed with me, I started going into dancing. And all of a sudden those doubts went. I don't know where they went to, but they weren't there any more! I felt myself right in the presence of God, just like that! Speaking in the Spirit, Miss Black let me know that I was righteous before God. It came as quite a shock to me – but I felt myself in the presence of God, worshipping before the King. While I was still standing she prophesied about the daughter of the King, and the mantle of righteousness, and all of a sudden I knew it was for me.[3] The doubts haven't been there since, and there has been a presence of God with me that wasn't there before. I have been able to worship God in a new freedom, in the knowledge that I am righteous before God. I praise God that the doubts have gone now and I am free to carry on in His calling.

Having once been in a denomination known for its resistance to Pentecost, I could appreciate something of Carolyn's problem. There had been a time when God spoke to me very clearly: 'Lean not on your own understanding.'

I thought, 'Lord, I'm not leaning on my own understanding.'

But I had the religious understanding of generations in my blood, and attitudes that were very strongly held. One day God came and set me free. He cleansed my mind, that I might have the mind of Christ and leave all prejudice behind me.

God, the heavenly physician, looks down on you and me and sees exactly what we require. The truth is that many of us do not have a clear, accurate knowledge of our spiritual condition. We may be aware that we are not very happy or that we tend to get upset easily, but we do not know the extent of our infections or diseases in the spiritual realm. Now the heavenly doctor knows us altogether. He knows both the difficulties that we are aware of and those of which we are not aware. We might, for example, suffer from a physical disease. But it may be that the physical condition is rooted in certain negative attitudes such as bitterness or resentment. Naturally we want physical healing. God, on the other hand, wants to go to the cause of the disease, and He goes right to the bottom. The entertainment of any form of sin, such as lack of forgiveness, is very dangerous from a physical point of view, apart altogether from a spiritual point of view.

God wants to do this fundamental work in us: to bring revival that touches to the very depth of being. We can have a noisy revival or a quiet revival, so long as the work is done one way or the other, that we be changed to the very depth of our beings.

How far has this to go?

It has to go to that point where our life is giving a pure reflection of the Lord Jesus Christ. It has not to stop short of that by a hairbreadth. It has to go to the point where people looking at us are seeing Christ in us, and listening to us are hearing the word of Christ. They are seeing His strength, His meekness, His kindness, His boldness. Ultimately Christ wants a church that not only reflects these characteristics, but through which the power of God comes surging as it came through the Lord Jesus in the days of His flesh. He wants to change us into the likeness of Christ. He came that we might have life more abundantly. It is the emancipation not just 'from' but 'into' – upward and out of the present condition into the glory of God. And we are not going fully there until we are fully changed. None of us is going to trick God. We are not going into that deep place carrying all the baggage of our own choosing. 'I don't want to let this or that go ... That TV programme is not a good one, I know, but there are interesting bits in it, and it has a story line – I don't want that to go ... And I really have a right to be angry at So-and-so – Lord, you know what he did to me, and I'll never forget it, I was so deeply hurt, and I can't let that go.'

'Well, don't bother coming for ministry,' is my response. As the professor once wrote on the back of a fellow student's essay, 'This is a waste of your time, my time, and God's time.' Unless you are prepared to be changed where the change is needed, there is no point in seeking ministry.

The aim is not merely a pleasant spiritual experience. Rather let the cry in your heart be, 'O God, change me. I've seen the shine of the glory of God on other faces, and I want to reflect His glory. I want to get rid of the baggage that has lain in the bottom of my life for years. I want to be totally open with God, and let Him probe to the inner recess of my being. I want truth in the inward parts – even if it hurts.' As with Graham and the others also, it is often at the point of pain that one breaks through into that realm of utter reality.

Notes

1. A 'tarry' meeting is one intended for the deepening of spiritual life. It is so named from Christ's command to His disciples to 'tarry' in Jerusalem until they were filled with the Holy Spirit.

2. In her message to Alistair, Elizabeth Austin had also spoken (this was the 'nice' bit!) of an anointing on his life and of God's intention to use him more. This seemed to come to fruition in the following way. Having had a longstanding burden for the lost, for some years Alistair had been involved with outreach among Muslims, but latterly had met a shut door so far as evangelistic opportunities were concerned. However, shortly after the experiences described here, he felt a fairly clear leading to launch out in open-air evangelism, using a sketch board. He now goes with a team into Glasgow city centre at least once a month.

3. The theme of the prophecy was possibly based on Psalm 45.

Chapter 8

And the Walls Came Tumbling Down

Ronnie, whose story appeared a few pages back, was a comparatively young Christian; the wall that he faced was all too evident to him, and he had to punch his way through it. **Owen**, by contrast, was a Christian of many years' standing, and the wall that God showed him had stood there impregnable and unsuspected until God Himself effectively demolished it. Mature and gifted beyond the ordinary, for years Owen had led one of our branch churches (subsequently integrated into the church in Greenock).[1] His love for Christ was deep and passionate.

Walls of Tradition

And yet ... recent events in the church of Christ had not met with his undiluted approval. Strongly attached to the traditions of worship and evangelism in which he himself had been nourished, he was apt to be critical of any radical departure from these. Ironically, it was at just such a gathering that the Spirit swept in and demolished the structure of prejudice that had hampered his own growth in God and his ministry to others. The change had not been entirely sudden; through the advent of the new ministry in our own fellowship in November 1994 God had been quietly disarming His servant over a number of

97

months. But the final stage was dramatic for all that, and its fruits were clearly witnessed by those of us who heard him speak in April 1995 shortly after the event:

> I am excited at what God has been doing, and there is a tremendous anticipation upon my spirit over what He will do in these last moments of time. A scene from *The Last Battle* by C.S. Lewis expresses my own condition very aptly. There was a door to be passed through into the land of Aslan, who represents Christ. A very beautiful land, it had a different effect on individuals as they passed through the door after the final battle had been fought. To the dwarves crouching just inside, everything good tasted of straw and dust. (None of us figure we're the dwarves.) Others went through the door with bewilderment, amazed at what they were seeing. Still others were filled with joy, and sought to go 'higher up and further in!' – there was no time to hang about the door.
>
> And that is the desire of my heart. I am rejoicing over the miraculous work God has done in me over very recent days. I came in contact with some very good servants of God, honest men, moving deeply with God but encountering tremendous criticism. The flow of the life of God coming through them was very similar to what we are experiencing here, but it is strongly resisted by the established and other churches – evangelical, charismatic, pentecostal. And it all ties in with what I have to say.
>
> God is moving despite the great walls of resistance that we build up. We don't like to think we are traditional or in a rut; God has to show it to us. We are very proud of our spirituality, and God is breaking down pride, humbling His church in very practical ways – bringing us down on the carpet. Sometimes the significance may be no more than that we have been obedient; we may not encounter a deep spiritual experience the first few occasions. But what

is happening is that there is a yielding to God, a softening within, and a preparedness to go with God.

In relation to what we have heard from Mexico, why do these things happen in other countries?[2] Why in less educated, less sophisticated societies? People haven't learned to become 'knowledgeable' in their religion, to build up an impression of themselves, their movements and their churches. They are in great need; their lifestyle is very simple. And because of their need they hear a word from God and they believe it. Inherent within many people from Latin countries is a desire to worship, much stronger than in other parts of the western world. And they're a little more naive too – I wish we were all as naive as they. When somebody they trust says, 'These signs shall follow them who believe,' they actually believe that.

Another dimension

The gentlemen of whom I spoke were very self-effacing but had a great deal to offer, moving very powerfully with God. The meeting was exceptionally informal, with a total avoidance of 'hype'. It began very quietly, in an orderly way. But there was something different: a something in the atmosphere that touched me very deeply. There was a reality that I recognized (we know it here). God had been working in my own heart, but I had not fully come through. I had become traditional and rigid, and God had to break this rigidity down. He has begun to work on pride and to break down resistances.

I beheld an unusual phenomenon that night. One of the criticisms levelled against these men is that people are struck dumb in their meetings. The orthodox pentecostal or charismatic attitude is that when you are given the opportunity to testify about Jesus you should be speaking. There's an awful lot of talk in the church; now many of us are learning to be silent and do a little bit more listening. One of those present was the pastor of a very big church in Texas. Highly articulate, he had a wonderful teaching ministry and in ordinary conversation could talk the hind legs off a donkey. Asked to tell the company what God had done for him, he stood silent, unable to speak. And there was an awe across the company.

The leader of the meeting said, 'Do you realize that in the time that he has been silent looking across this company with an anointing on him, this man has said more than many say in sermons that come from the head?'

And that was true.

The same thing happened with another, and there was great laughter. A couple of young lads at my back who were just in off the street thought this was rather amusing, so they were laughing too – not in the Spirit, obviously, but they were having a good time! At the end of the meeting the same young lads, who had no thought about God and were only there to disrupt, were lying on their backs on the floor like little lambs. They experienced the power of the risen Lord.

All of this did not unsettle me in the slightest; the balance of reverence and humour appealed to me. I sensed a reality, and I sensed something coming down within me: God was disarming me, and my resistance was ebbing away. I was in another dimension; I can still feel it. Traditionalism and formalism were out the window. It was very relaxed, and the Spirit of the Lord was having freedom to move as He would. Unusual things were happening: there was a wind in the place, a spiritual wind blowing across the company. It was beautiful.

The preaching was powerful in a relaxed fashion – like Mr Black's, very laid back and easy to listen to. The speaker was an extremely mature Christian of many years' standing, and I believe that that development in his preaching has only taken place over comparatively few years since entering into this deeper life in God.

But it is this other dimension that I am trying to get across: a dimension that I for one had been missing while others were entering in. But I became aware of it on that occasion. It is easily missed, this other dimension. You won't miss it if your heart is humble, if you are open and have no preconceived notions, if you are pliable in the hand of God and seeking God. It was like that in the Welsh revival. Many of those instrumental in the Welsh revival were young – which would suggest immaturity. It's as though God has to pass by the so-called mature because they become rigid and immovable. They think they are being faithful to God, when all the time His presence is receding. He will not let you live in that little world of yours within a world, as Myers puts it.[3] Your little backwater will become stagnant. The glory and the power of Christ – even what you have – will recede.

I want to tell you what happened to me. While still on the platform, the pastor looked over at me and said, 'Don't go away. I want to pray with you.' Normally I don't allow just anybody to do that; but he was particularly trustworthy and pure, and there was a Christ-like radiance about the man's face. He had a very unusual style, which had nothing to do with being American. The sense of the wind blowing in the place was real; people were going down before it. (I feel it tonight in this place. The atmosphere is pregnant with the power and the glory of Christ.)

When I was prayed for, I went backwards very fast. What threw me back was a spiritual spout of water. Odd as it might sound, I saw it. You may have seen an oil well being drilled: when oil is struck it comes up as a gusher. That's exactly the word that came to me: 'It's a gusher!' I could see it in my spirit clearly as I went down. The power of God finds its way through the hard bedrock of our lives: isn't that an amazing miracle?

Two days later in the early hours of the morning God showed me, again in picture form, what He had to break through: a brick wall of immense thickness, with a massive crack right over the cross-section of it.

I said, 'Lord, what is this?'

He said, 'Defences.'

The wall represented my defences, my resistances. And there was a gaping crack right down it. He demolished it! It was real, wonderfully real.

I feel as though I have passed through that door into Aslan's land.

To those who are protesting, hanging on to the past and saying, 'It was wonderful there, Lord; I remember all the experiences I had over there – I want to go back there for a little while!' He is saying, 'Oh, no, no, no. I don't stop; I'm moving on! Are you coming?'

He waited for me; wonderful Jesus waited for me, as He waits for you. And if you don't come? He says, 'You won't lose your salvation, no. But in that day when you meet My eyes [Oh, Master!] and you haven't done what I called you to do, what will you say then?' An intolerable moment.

God is separating out His sanctified ones for the last great conflict, and He is looking for volunteers, not conscripts. The call of God is going out in these last days. The brilliant, majestic Son of God is gone forth to smite the enemy of souls. We can be part of this great work of God in these latter days, or we can be flotsam and jetsam on the banks of the great river of God.

One thing God has made quite clear to me: this is the day of signs and wonders. Christ's promise that *these signs shall follow the preaching of the word* is going to be gloriously fulfilled. *Greater works than these shall ye do*, saith Jesus. But our eyes will not be on the works, amazing as they are. You can't exist on the miracles in themselves; the joy that they give is passing. They will only really be meaningful to you if Christ is the centre of your life. These are the beautiful gifts that come from the hands of Jesus and bear His fragrance. *All day long My hands are stretched out to you* (Isaiah 65:2). All day long? And we walk about in poverty, powerless, despondent, putting-a-front-on Christians, when God would have us to be radiant, moving in the power of the eternal God, walking with triumphant Jesus.

Owen then spoke of something that had happened a few hours earlier when we had prayed together:

The occasion when I was with Mr Black this morning is one I will never forget. It was so spontaneous, so beautiful. All of a sudden the presence of the glory of Christ came near, and as he was praying for me there came a mist of the glory of God between. It wasn't a bright light; it was like a cloud of dew, each droplet suffused with light. We were enclosed in a cloud of glory. It was so beautiful.

Owen found that his preaching was affected by his recent experiences:

In the matter of preaching, I sense that God wants to do something. We always like to say, 'I have God's word, given by Him,' but I for one have to ask, 'How often has God given?' And He is saying that this will change. It is not seeking sermons, but seeking God, finding out the mind of the Spirit. And what came tonight came in a very unusual way. For some reason over the last week or so I'm beginning to see pictures in front of me. I'm not normally given to this sort of thing. But I do know they are of God. In the present instance all texts went out of my mind. And there came in front of me a sheet of some material that was full of perforations. I sensed this was God showing me something, but I didn't understand what I was looking at.

I said, 'What is that?'

He said, 'That is lives that cannot hold what I have given, lives that have become sieves.'

The sermon that Owen went on to preach was marked by an unusual anointing, searching and yet gracious, seasoned by humour. He made an interesting observation:

In the midst of all that has been happening recently, do you know what I actually heard? I heard Christ laugh. That may seem strange, yet it was the most beautiful thing. It was the most manly laugh I have ever heard. I have heard Satan laugh – so horrible was it that through all the years I shall never forget it. But when I heard Christ laugh, oh! it was wonderful, it was rich, strong, deep and glorious. There was a singing in it, a joy and victory in it. So you may laugh! A saving sense of humour is a very good thing. It is not true that if you want to be a saint of God you shouldn't have a sense of humour.

Firm in the assurance of Christ's working in his own life, he encouraged his audience:

You cannot change yourself, but there is One that can penetrate the granite of that personality. Can He mellow that proud spirit? Yes, He can. One of the chief sins within the church today is pride. 'Why do some people make strange noises? What do they achieve? ... How ridiculous I look lying on the floor laughing!' There are many spiritual experiences we may have, depending on whether we are prepared to give ourselves over to them. Sometimes they come irresistibly: they are spontaneously wonderful. But God will never push His way into your life. Christ is the perfect gentleman: 'Behold I stand at the door and knock. Open to Me, My beloved. See if I will not pour out for you a blessing.'

The change that Owen experienced on the occasion which he has described was no flash in the pan. The months of the new ministry had been an essential preparation for it, and when God cracked open the wall of his child's defences the transformation was immediate, evident and lasting. The spiritual ministry that had been his flowed with an enhanced grace and power; gone was the critical spirit that had hindered his appreciation of new ways of God's working. In the years that have followed he has gone from strength to strength, a true minister of the fragrance and the victory of Christ.

A Walled Garden

The representation of spiritual truth in vivid pictorial form comes to some people more than others. One who was used to 'seeing things in pictures' was **Rhian**, who also had the music of her Welsh mother's people in her blood. Whereas the wall in Owen's experience appeared to him when it was well-nigh demolished, Rhian's experience started with a picture:

I saw a garden on my right-hand side. Standing outside, I could see it was enclosed with a wall. I knew that in the garden there was fruit and water, and that it was a place of absolute abundance: the branches of fruit were coming over the wall. Anybody walking outside that garden could pick the fruit off the branches and be fed. In my own mind I tried to work out what all of that meant, but nothing really came of it, and I just forgot about it. And then one night maybe a week later I started to read from the Song of Songs, where the bride is described as a garden enclosed, and it was exactly what I had seen.

I was aware that God was speaking to me and giving revelation. He was bringing to my consciousness a part in me that I didn't even know was there, and it was as if He had to bring it to mind by using this means. He was making me aware that there was a need in myself. I knew that deep down in my being there was something like a wall. There was a part that was closed to other people, and closed to God. I think the reason for this was that as a teenager, just to get by in the world, I had made a very conscious decision that I wasn't going to get hurt by people and had put up a barrier. That probably had affected me much more deeply than I realized. But God was now touching this part and bringing it back to my consciousness.

The morning after I had read the passage from the Song of Songs, when I picked up the daily reading book by my bed, it spoke of a bottle that was corked so that the fragrance of the ointment couldn't get out. God spoke to me again and said, 'That's like you! You are stopping something inside yourself; you are stopping part of your love to Christ from flowing out because you are keeping it all hidden deep down inside, and you are not letting His love come into that part of your being so that you can love Him back in return.'

I wrote a note to Miss (Mary) Black explaining what I was feeling. In every meeting I became more aware of this part in me. Though I had been down on the floor a few times, I knew that God wasn't getting all the way into the deeps, and that there was something not quite right.

A few nights later Miss Black prayed with me where I sat. It was as if a torrent of light came in and started to shake up and loosen that place inside me. God was beginning the work. On the following Monday night when Miss Black gave the appeal, I began to feel the anointing of God coming on me.

I wondered, 'Should I just sit here and take in what God is already doing? . . . No, I'll take the risk and go forward.'

She prayed with me and I went down. While I was down Mrs Gault came over and prayed with me as well. As she did so, something broke. There came a freedom deep down inside, and I felt an absolute overflow of joy. Apparently I started to laugh, though I didn't know it at the time. But I just knew there was a release and a sense of freedom. That part which had become like a knot inside me was gone in a moment: it was completely gone. I felt like a totally different person. Waking the next morning I could hardly believe it: I felt so different inside, and so free. I was amazed that Christ could do that, amazed that even when I hadn't been conscious of the problem in my life, He began to make me conscious of it so that He could deal with it. And He dealt with it in a moment of time: it wasn't a case of a little bit being taken away every time I was on the floor. In an instant Christ came and completely changed me. I feel brand new, absolutely changed inside. It's as though a doorway into God has opened to me, and I have a whole land to explore in God, a land of freedom, abundance and absolute joy.

Speaking of the preparation for this experience a few weeks later, Rhian commented, 'God made it very clear to me it would only be Christ who would come into that enclosed area of my life. There would be no pain or disillusionment, because He wouldn't hurt me. But in letting Him in there would be more love for other people, the love of Christ flowing out from myself to them.' She added that the barrier had not returned, and alluded to a conversation she had had with my daughter Grace:

Mrs Gault said an interesting thing to me. She told me that she had prayed with me for a number of years, and every time she had felt Christ coming in love really deep down into me, and I in turn was opening up deeply; yet there was always this bit that to her disappointment never opened. But when she went to pray with me on the occasion when I was lying on the floor the barrier was gone. She called it an absolute miracle: she was aware that, although people had been ministering to me, that sort of thing had never been touched until then. Praise His Name.

God continued to work deeply in Rhian's life following this experience of March 1995. Testifying at the beginning of 1996 to what He had done for her in the previous year, she said:

I have found a real deepening of God. I feel as though I am a different person at the end of 1995 from what I was at the beginning, and that God has worked a very deep change through the ministry that has come into the church, and through His own dealing with me. One part of the New Year word that has really lived for me is that 'if you are willing and obedient you will eat the good of the land'.[4]

The Breaking of the Will

She touched at this point on an extremely significant stage in her spiritual development. This occurred later in the year:

One area that God has dealt with this year is my will. For many years I thought my will had been broken to God, but I came to the realization, which was quite horrific at the time, that my will wasn't broken, and it was my own will that was willing me to do the will of God. It was not until He brought into my life a situation which was too strong for me that I realized that at that cross I needed to break and that there my will would be truly broken. I have found that instead of my own determination to do what God wants me to do, there is inside me a determination that is of God and that He has placed in me. A fundamental change of character has come with the inflow of the life of Christ. I am finding that I am totally free to do what God wants me to do: there is no longer any struggle at all with trying to will myself to do the will of God, but just a sweetness and an ease in following what God wants. Over the whole year there has been that sense of blessing and of the deepening of the anointing of God, and a moving forward in the realm of battle too.

She explained that the kind of change that took place at that point was one she had thought impossible, because it involved what she had taken to be her essential nature. It was a revelation to her that this thing she had thought was an inseparable part of her being was in fact an unbroken will. She needed, and received, a real deliverance from its binding power.

Not only her own life benefited from these events. Already deeply involved in pastoral work with students at the college where she herself graduated as an occupational therapist, she has become increasingly fruitful in communicating the life of Christ to them and to many others.

Walls of defence

The imagery of defensive walls occurred again in the testimony of **Sue C**, an experienced nurse and a willing helper in many aspects of church life. Like many others, she had gone forward for ministry more than once. She describes the first occasion:

I was very awed when the new ministry first started in our church. Deeply wanting to be a part of it, I was nevertheless afraid of two things: first, would anyone be able to **catch** me! and, second, what would happen when I was 'down'?

Some time elapsed before I plucked up the courage to go forward. It was at the end of a meeting, when people were beginning to go home – I felt it would be less conspicuous that way. I suppose I didn't want to 'embarrass' myself during the meeting.

I have often felt during my Christian life that I was a 'no-user' and a bit of a failure in Christ's eyes. Yet my desire has always been to be in the place that God has chosen for me, and I have always had a hunger in my heart for the deeper things of God.

Standing there in front of Alison Speirs (who was ministering to me), I knew I had a choice to make: either to concentrate on what was going to happen, or to let my whole being be focused on Christ. I chose the latter and was so overcome with the presence of the love of Christ that overwhelmed me that before I knew it I was lying on the floor.

I remained there very quietly, knowing that it was a very special moment for me. I felt I was resting in the lovely arms of Christ, and He was reassuring me, as a tender parent would a child, of His deep love for me. He spoke to me in words of tenderness and beauty, showing me that I wasn't the person **I** thought I was. He showed me how **He** saw me, words which could not even be easily written down on paper.

I was a 'fearing child' before going for ministry, but the end of it found me in a much deeper place with 'the One whom my soul loveth'.

The experience of Christ's love is wonderful, but our continuing communion with him is deeply contested. Sue later found a barrier had arisen that she needed help to overcome:

After suffering a deep wound of hurt I began to put defences up in my life, to the point where I found it very hard to enter deeply into a meeting. The hurt would rise and cause me to weep whenever I reached that deep place in Christ which I loved. I felt so 'undone' in that place that I began to hold back and not allow myself to go there. After three weeks of this I was very wearied of it and knew something had to be done. I knew it was wrong to put up these defensive walls, but I felt overtaken and unable to do anything about it.

One Saturday night it seemed right to go out for ministry. Feeling rather exposed lying on my back at the front of the platform (for this was a private meeting between my God and me), I surveyed the area around me and turned face down so as to allow this privacy of being. God began to do a deep healing work in me and caused the walls I had put up to come down. In the doing of this He has created a place of deep peace and beauty and stillness in my being.

It has caused me to see the foolishness of putting up those defences, and I don't want to go back there again. I know that this 'new place' will be an ongoing work, but, praise God, it has begun, and through difficulty and pain there can come healing and wholeness.

Walls of tradition, walls of prejudice, walls of defence – whatever they are, Christ can dismantle them when we give Him the chance. It is vitally important that we do not rest in past 'experiences', wonderful though they may be. The times of revelation are given to spur us on our journey. Like the apostle Paul we press on, looking not backwards but forwards. The door of hope is forever open, as the next chapter illustrates.

Notes

1. Owen Martin appears in my book *Christ the Deliverer* (New Dawn Books, 1991), chapter 6, in connection with a healing from blindness that occurred spontaneously under his ministry.

2. See chapter 2.
3. Never at even, pillowed on a pleasure,
   Sleep with the wings of aspiration furled,
   Hide the last mite of the forbidden treasure,
   Keep for myself a world within the world...
         (From F.W.H. Myers, *Saint Paul*)
4. The New Year word for 1995 was from Isaiah 1:18–19 and Psalm 132:13–16.

Chapter 9

A Door of Hope

Therefore, behold, I will allure her, and bring her into the wilderness, and speak tenderly unto her. And I will give her her vineyards there, and the Valley of Achor [troubling] for a door of hope; and she shall sing there, as in the days of her youth.   (Hosea 2:14–15)[1]

'Well, it's back home to the realities of washing, ironing, weeding,' wrote **Linda B** some weeks after her return from our July camp in 1997. 'However,' she continued,

I feel very deeply affected by my few days at camp and as I write I feel a Presence abiding within me and a peace such as I have never felt before...

What I wasn't prepared for was the way in which God was calling me closer to Him. I had anticipated something less gentle; perhaps even a degree of deliverance was what I was expecting. Instead God exposed my deepest hurts and smoothed a healing balm on them...

Tuesday, July 15th would have been mum's sixty-ninth birthday. My sister Pauline and I spoke briefly that morning about the significance of the day and then I dropped the subject. But God did not want it to be dismissed so lightly. In fact it was on the

113

following evening that Pauline [in preaching] referred to the dark months during my father's illness and following his death. Those were dark days for me too, both on a natural and spiritual level. I have never experienced any difficulty in admitting to myself the depth of my suffering with regard to the death of my father in particular, but I cannot bear to look upon those months that Pauline kept referring to. There is only one other period in my life that causes me as much anguish – much more anguish, in fact: the loss of our first baby whom I miscarried at three months and whose birthday would have been July 9th. Thirteen years on, I could not think about that precious life without tremendous pain and scarcely a day went by without my thoughts turning in that direction. There was no bitterness, no resentment, no questioning why – just a sense of loss, pain, grief. But when you prayed with me on the last night of camp, Mr Black, I quite clearly, almost audibly heard God whisper in my ear that He would always be at my side, that even though my parents and my child had to leave me relatively early in my years, He would never ever leave me, had never left me and had always loved me. I felt like a baby snuggled up in a shawl, all warm and safe and secure and at peace.

What have I learned from this as time has allowed it all to sink in? I think that over the past 15 years I have built a wall around myself to a certain extent. Perhaps wall is too strong a word – certainly a barrier of some sort, so that I [would] not be as hurt as I was when I was separated from those closest to me. Unfortunately my barrier served to keep at arms' length the One who desired to be closest to me, whose love and comfort I needed and longed for so desperately, whose love I was aware of at one level but without truly knowing it as I ought.

It is very difficult to express such deep, personal feelings, and I don't think I've conveyed clearly how

God touched me during camp and in the days which have followed. However, I trust you will have glimpsed some of it and extend my thanks to Mary (to whom you can show this letter if it makes any sense at all) who was used very deeply by God to speak to me with startling clarity in her preaching... [2]

Thank you from the bottom of my heart for being there for us so selflessly.

Linda.

As many of my readers will know, a fearful scar can be left on the mother who has lost a baby. Fathers often fail to understand how deep and serious this can be. They often have no real bond with the child till after birth, when identity has developed. The mother, on the other hand, has been conscious of identity from very early stages of pregnancy. The way in which God healed Linda from the effects of this miscarriage was connected for me with a revelation of truth that had come in a context that was both like and unlike Linda's situation.

Abortion

Some years ago a gentleman came to me for help. He had found a barrier in his spiritual life: there was a point past which he could make no progress. We spoke around the subject for a little time, and quite casually he mentioned an abortion his daughter had undergone some time earlier. He indicated that he and his wife had encouraged and fully supported her in the matter. He then passed on to speak of other things.

I immediately interrupted him and objected: 'But that was murder. Do you realize what you have done? You are guilty of murdering your own flesh and blood, and moreover you will meet that child one day.'

He was shocked.

'Yes,' I said, 'I mean it. That is the truth in the eyes of God.'

He completely broke and bitterly repented. God met him with gracious deliverance, and he was set totally free. His wife then had to go through exactly the same process. Both their lives were revolutionized.

The fact that the world, even perhaps some sections of the professed Christian world, looks lightly on abortion, in no way alters the law of God. He dealt severely though very mercifully with my friends – they had to face the truth.

It is an old and true saying that circumstances alter cases, and in a second case the approach has been different, with wonderful consequences.

Very early in life a young person became pregnant, and strong pressures were brought on her by family and friends to have an abortion. She would have loved to find a way out of this, but it seemed impossible. Having no Christian background, she went through with the termination and ever after carried pain and guilt. Although later she was happily married, the wound remained unhealed. Even after she had become a Christian and received her baptism in the Spirit, the pain was still there, and one day she came to me for help. Her revelation was a shock to me. I had had no idea that anything like that had happened in her earlier days.

And then God came in an amazingly gracious way. I had no need or desire to say, 'You are a murderer.' She knew her sin and needed no harsh words of mine to bring it home to her. She needed love. She needed healing, and suddenly I felt God gave me revelation.

I said, 'For years you have carried this burden, and every time you think of this child [I think it was a girl] there is a barrier of guilt between you and her because of what you did. Now God wants to take away the barrier. The child is in His hands and the blood of Christ is there for your forgiveness.' She accepted God's offer, and I showed her how the child was growing into adulthood in heaven, and she would meet her again: and not only that – but as God had forgiven her, so would her daughter. I suddenly realized powerfully that my friend could now release her love for the daughter whom she had lost, and she did. She came into glory. I was personally thrilled at what God did.

But not only that. I was then able to speak of this lovely truth to others, and it has brought such comfort and joy. Not only does it apply where there has been abortion, but part of it applies where there has been miscarriage. And so in Linda's case the hidden unhealed pain surfaced and God showed her how the child was growing and prospering on the other side and would meet her as a maturing adult one day in the presence of Christ. She was free to love and know that she would be loved. It has had a wonderful effect on her spiritual life.

It is my hope and prayer that if any reader has been carrying a burden in this realm they too will find the healing of God.

Postnatal Depression

Those who have never borne a child may have little or no conception of how serious can be the condition now known as postnatal depression. In the case of **Heather**,[3] it took the deep and sustained ministry of the Spirit to work the miracle that brought her gloriously out of the black pit that she found herself in. Testifying in December 1996 she explained:

> My problem goes back eighteen months to the birth of my youngest child. It was a traumatic birth, delayed for so long that my body went into shock. After being rushed in for an emergency Caesarean I was given a blood transfusion and went into intensive care. The doctors told me afterwards that it was touch and go. But the thing that hit me most was that I wasn't a Christian at the time: I was a backslider. To think that I was nearly in hell was horrible.
>
> I came out of hospital only to be rushed back in with a haemorrhage. As the days went on, I went into

a postnatal depression – a condition you need to experience to understand its indescribable blackness and horror. Not knowing at the time what was wrong with me, I simply felt that I couldn't cope with life in general. It was another visit to the doctor that revealed I had both postnatal depression and post-traumatic stress syndrome.

Mrs Gault prayed with me one Sunday night in Greenock. I felt God touched me physically: there was a tingling sensation over the back of my neck, and I went home quite happily. But the next day was the worst I had ever had, like a backlash. Things got a bit easier as the week wore on, until the Saturday night came and Mr Black invited us to come forward for ministry. Now I had always been afraid of **not** going down when prayed for (though this should not have been a problem, for God can meet you when you are standing). There had been a previous occasion when I had felt to go out but had not done so. When I had told Mrs Gault that I had resisted going, she had said, 'Don't ever do that, because that's God calling you.' And so this time I got up off my seat and raced to the front! I did go prostrate ... it was like waves and waves and waves of light that God brought upon me.

Yet on the Sunday morning I felt so terrible again that as soon as I arrived at church I went up the back stairs into the ladies' room and broke my heart. Then I wandered outside for a little. By the time I went into the meeting, my eyes were sunk into my head with crying that would not stop.

Floods of tears continued as Mrs Gault ministered to me. Just as she was walking away I saw myself in vision standing in the darkness of a gully with mountains round about me. There was a light at the top, but I couldn't reach it. Even though I was better for the rest of the day, by the time of the evening service I sensed there was still something not right. So

I said to my sister Elaine, 'I feel there's something that has to be removed from me.'

Mrs Gault took us both into the vestry. When we started to pray, I felt a darkness hanging over my right shoulder. As I went out into God, I was less aware of Elaine and Mrs Gault sitting there, and there came an explosion. The whole lot of it went! It was tremendous. It's hard to describe, but I got to the light, I really did – I got to that light that I had been wanting to reach, and God totally healed me. I'm just longing to go back to the doctor and tell her that I have no need of the anti-depressants she had intended to prescribe, for I'm healed!

Only the God who created and breathed life into us can reach so fundamentally into the recesses of the human psyche and transform grief into joy, bringing light from darkness.

Childhood Scars

This was the testimony also of **John**, who had had a wonderful salvation from a life of drug abuse. By the time we knew him he was working for Teen Challenge at The Haven, Kilmacolm. But there were unhealed wounds deep within, as he began to reveal when he sought help in 1996 because of family circumstances the detail of which he did not reveal. When he received prayer at this point he may have thought that this was substantially all he needed. If so, a surprise awaited him:

It was the next day that I discovered what this was all leading up to. God wanted to deal with something in my own past. That Sunday morning in the Port Glasgow church, Joan invited those wanting ministry to step out into the aisles.[4] God was moving, and I felt a deep stirring within me. It was then that God (I believe) spoke to me and said, 'Yesterday the abuse of your family was dealt with, but what about the abuse that happened to you?'

Moving out into the aisle, I was overwhelmed by the power of God. I could sense someone coming towards me, but before anyone came near me I fell back. No human hand touched me, though I praise God for the people who appeared behind to catch me.

Lying on the floor, I felt as though my whole body was shaking. Tears began to stream down the side of my face as I felt God speaking again and saying, 'I have forgiven you much. Can you forgive this one who abused you?'

I cried, 'God, give me the grace to forgive this person.'

At this point I went right out in the Spirit, and what happened next is hard to describe. I was filled, I believe, with the very compassion of Christ. Not only was I able to forgive, but I found myself crying for the salvation of this person's soul.

Now, early in 1997, the Lord is still bringing fruit out of this. He has shown me defects in my character that were caused by the events of the past.

I had begun to notice that there were certain people I found it hard to get on with and hard to talk to. I also noticed that most of them were in positions of leadership or authority. I went before God and said, 'Lord, these weaknesses are not of You. Show me why they are there and how to get rid of them. I know this is hindering my walk with you, and I long for all hindrances to be removed.'

God is faithful; He answered me. He was present in the time of need and showed me two things.

One of them was the incident of abuse mentioned above. Because it had taken place while I was somewhere I should not have been, I would not tell anyone for fear of getting into trouble. I was about seven or eight years old at this time. After the incident, I would be standing at a bus stop or at the local shops with my mum and dad when the person concerned would go past, but although I cringed at the sight, I still could not open up to anyone about it.

The second circumstance involved my family. My mother, who was alcoholic, would turn very nasty with drink. On several occasions she would round on me and say, 'Your father is not your father – you're nothing but a little bastard.' When sober, she would apologize for what she had said. But these thoughts always came back to haunt me ... 'Is my dad really my dad – or is someone else my dad?' As a child I did not know what to believe.

The main problem arising from both of these situations was that I developed a lack of trust for those in authority around me and found it increasingly hard to share things with them. The wall of non-communication seemed to grow thicker and thicker, till it came to the point where I bottled everything up and shared nothing with anyone.

I believe that when God gives me the strength to share these things, as I am doing now, He is proving faithful and true to His word and giving evidence that I can overcome the difficulties that have held me back for so long. *And they overcame him by the blood of the Lamb, and by the word of their testimony* (Revelation 12:11).

To return to the incident in the Port Glasgow church, when I eventually rose from the floor everyone had gone home apart from Joan, who was waiting to lock up, and one other who had stayed behind to drive me home. I couldn't say how long I was there, but what I can say is that time meant nothing, and I left with my mourning turned to joy. The glory belongs to God and Him alone.

Door into Joy

A door into joy opened also for **Carol D**, a student training to be a primary teacher. Under the influence of

Andrew and Rhian (chapters 6 and 8) she had found Christ and been baptized in the Spirit during the previous eighteen months, but at the time of our summer camps in 1995 she began to feel the need of something more:

> In the meetings I was feeling the presence of God and was getting through to a measure, but out of the meetings I was beginning to have reactions and not know where they were coming from. I really needed more of God to live the Christian life.
>
> The people I spoke to at first told me to go away and get really desperate and so forth! But by the time of the August camp Alison Speirs advised me to stop focusing on the problem: when God brought something to the surface, then it would be dealt with.
>
> So I tried to forget all about it and just find God in whatever I was doing, outside as well as inside meetings. And it was going fine – but I still had a desire in me to know a lot more of God and wasn't getting very far in finding it. At the college we had been encountering opposition, basically to Pentecost but to Struthers as well, and it was pretty tough to do anything. It had been taking everything just to stand for Pentecost and for what we knew to be right. So I felt I hadn't been going forward at all, but simply standing.
>
> Although I was looking forward to the meeting in the college last Thursday night, I went without any sense of desperation or expectation of anything major happening to me. At the start of the meeting, I was just trying to get through to God. Andrew came over and began praying with me. It was all very gentle at first. Then before I knew it – unaware of my surroundings or of God being there – I was on the floor, and Rhian was praying with me as well!
>
> 'Oh, no,' I thought as I heard myself shouting. 'I'm getting deliverance!'

I didn't know what the deliverance was from or what was going on, or what anyone else in the meeting was doing. That was all I was aware of.

I just tried to push through it. I didn't care what was going on right at that moment; I just wanted to get back through to God again. The next thing I knew was that the shouting had stopped. I wasn't aware that Jesus had come, or that He had taken anything away, but I knew I was through it. Then as the meeting went on into singing, all I can remember feeling is an utter joy coming into me. People were smiling at me as I sat there with a huge grin on my face! But I didn't really mind, because there was such a presence of God there. What I had thought was joy was nothing compared to what I found now. It is hard to believe that I did not know what joy was. It was a pure joy that I had never known before, bringing with it amazing freedom; I felt wonderfully free of self. Even more amazing, the joy has stayed with me. I still don't know exactly what it was that God did – that's what I think the most amazing thing is: I don't know what it was that He took away! It was probably a part of self, something from the past that I never even knew was there; but all that really matters is that I have this joy. God has opened a door for me, but He had to touch that part deep inside and take it away before I could enter through that door into more of Him.

A week later God spoke to Carol from the verse ... *your sorrow shall be turned into joy* (John 16:20). This was the only clue she was given as to what He had done for her.

Carol's story is an encouragement to all who set themselves to 'follow on to know the Lord'. God saw her desire for Him; more than that, He saw the need that she could not see. It did not matter that she could not tell how He accomplished the miracle that brought her spiritual healing. What mattered, as she lay on the operating table of God, was that she co-operated with the One who knew exactly what He was doing.

Notes

1. The New Scofield Reference Bible (Authorized King James Version, ed. C.I. Scofield, DD, Oxford University Press, 1967).

2. A theme from Hosea had been very much in Linda's mind for days leading up to the July camp. She was not surprised when Mary preached on the verses that provide the title for this chapter (Hosea 2:14–15).

3. Heather is sister to Karen, the story of whose miraculous healing is in chapter 6.

4. Joan Jewell is minister of our Port Glasgow church. Her healing ministry is featured in my book *Revival: Living in the Realities* (New Dawn Books, 1993), chapter 9.

Chapter 10

God's Operating Table

When people began to realize the miraculous nature of what was happening to those who were falling prostrate under the hand of God, they responded in increasing numbers to the call for ministry. Sometimes as many as fifty to sixty went down. The reports that came back as to what God had done when they were before Him were both remarkable and encouraging. Wounds were healed at a very deep level, entanglements dissolved and sin convicted.

While to the casual eye it might seem that a large number of people responding to the same simple kind of ministry lay strewn in similar positions around the church floor, God's working within each life was highly individual. It is just as in a medical context, where one white-clad patient looks very like another when stretched out on the operating table – the apparent homogeneity does not prevent the surgeon from performing a very different operation on each! Although the testimonies to the 'new ministry' in this series of books have tended to be presented thematically, it can be refreshing to read a handful that are linked by little more than the fact of God's moving in this supernatural way. For this purpose I have selected a number of incidents from home and further afield, beginning with our New Year Conference in Greenock, 1995.

Of those who went forward for ministry there were some who wondered what was happening; if they fell on the floor they wondered if they should be there and why, and they were analysing everything that was going on all along the road. Then sometimes they got up and in spite of their ambivalence they had been healed of the thing for which they came. An encouraging instance was that of a mature Christian couple who came to our New Year Conference in 1995. **Colin** speaks first:

We came on Saturday night and heard much of how God had been blessing here with His presence, regarding this new anointing that had come upon Mr Black. God spoke to me and I had a great desire to come up higher in response to His invitation. I stood in the aisle with a bit of trepidation. But once I did this I got a great sense of peace, though not knowing what was going to happen. I had not been here in previous weeks and we had only been hearing what was on tape. As I stood in the aisle I was aware of people crowding around me. My mind was very much in gear, analysing things. I didn't really know what was happening. When Mr Black came to pray for me, I didn't know whether I should go down – the whole mind was very active. He came round a second time, and it was as he prayed on that occasion that, while my mind was still functioning, I knew there was something going on deeper within. As I looked to the Lord there was just that great sense that all the rest of you weren't here: you had all disappeared, and I didn't really want the meeting to end. But before I knew where I was the meeting was over, and I didn't know whether I had missed out or not.

I went and sat in a pew and wanted to stay there and abide for ever. Great words came somewhere deep inside, saying, 'All fear has gone,' and peace came to my soul. In these last few months there had been great anxiety and great fear of many things. But since that time as I sat quiet in the pew I have known that sense of the peace of God. I rejoice in having been here and gone through that experience, and would encourage anyone else who is in trepidation to step forth in faith. Our God is faithful to answer the cry of our hearts. I praise Him this afternoon that He answered mine.

Colin did not actually go down: God met him as he stood and sat. We are under no obligation to get into a rut. The important thing is to do what God impresses on us to do and not just follow a pattern. **Ann** did go down, though not without misgivings:

Over the last few months, I suppose, there has been an increasing hunger in my heart for the deeper things of God. And it hasn't been an easy few months. In fact it has been devastating. Many circumstances around our life have been pretty awful. Prior to this weekend many things had happened so that I was quite a sad person when I came, and yet I did know the love of Christ. When Mr Black preached, I responded to the call to go into the deeper things of God, to forsake self and the things that occupy us, even the things that are devastating to us. So I went out and stood worshipping the Lord in the usual way. And before I knew what had happened I was on the floor – I can only say that God put me on the floor, because there was no way I could have got there without God doing it!

In my mind I was very aware of everything around me and in many ways I felt very foolish laid on the floor, and yet I knew that I couldn't get up. Then I became aware that God was doing things at a much deeper level than the mind and even than the emotions; it was far deeper, though I didn't know what He was doing. At the same time through my mind there floated the thought, 'Well, people will think you are foolish down there!' But I still couldn't get up. Ultimately I did get up and sat in a pew. I knew that God was still at work, and that there were words coming from Him to my heart, such as, *In quietness and rest shall your strength be* [compare Isaiah 30:15]. I didn't really want to meet anybody after the meeting; I wanted to go away. I know that the work deep within is still going on: God is dealing and will deal with things that have to be changed. I know that I go away from this place a different person from the person who came in.

Colin's and Ann's testimonies were very down-to-earth. They spoke of God continuing to work: what He offered them was not a one-off experience, but a going into a way of life where the Holy Spirit had broken through and was continuing to operate.

The Perfect Physician

There was a tremendous joy in my spirit as I listened to such testimonies. In the past the pattern had been that I listened to people describing their problems while also listening to what God might be saying: I was in between, doing the best I could. But now I found myself totally relaxed and in a sense doing nothing, while those who came for ministry lay on the operating table of God, who knew all about them, including things they didn't know themselves. A perfect physician, He never botched an operation but did exactly what was needed in each case – and He was doing it all and doing it at the same time to a multiplied number of people. If you have never had hard work in this realm, you may not understand. But there are some of us who do understand something of the wonder of the action of God. You are not left conjecturing, 'I wonder if I've said the right thing ... I wonder if I've gone far enough in that.' Now you wonder nothing. You just say, 'O God, the anointing of the holy.'

The way in which these things happen brings no glory to man. I refuse to push people. Sometimes I felt sure, 'That one should be down on his back,' but I didn't want anyone to get up and say, 'You pushed me!' There were also times when a person went down before I even got to them. It works in different ways. It is not just the sensation of being on the floor that is vital. What is vital is your spirit breaking through into a new realm of freedom, and the Holy Spirit breaking through on you. There is a two-way traffic and an abiding in another dimension. It is a case of the great God coming very, very close to men – fearfully, gloriously close.

✣　✣　✣

Another who found inner healing early in 1995 was physiotherapist **Sue F**. She explains:

> For a long time I had been aware of pain inside. I didn't know what it was, only that it was there, deep down, an emotional or spiritual rather than a physical pain – though I could almost have doubled up with it. I had been very aware of it over the last seven years or so, but I now know that it had been there for longer than that. Since I wasn't very sure what it was, it was difficult for others to help me. I knew that God knew, but I wasn't convinced that He was actually going to do anything about it.
>
> I turned to a friend one night and said, 'Janet, I can't take any more. What is this?' [1]
>
> She said, 'I don't know.'
>
> But I felt a love coming through her that was not her own. It touched me, and I felt safe in having told her.

Some days later when Janet was reading a psalm and not thinking about Sue, God told her that the pain her friend was feeling was sorrow. She communicated this to Sue, who felt a peace come into her as she recognized the truth. She did not know why or how the sorrow had come to be there, but something inside her quickened, and she felt, 'God is going to do something about this.'

Sue began laughing as she said this. She continued:

I felt really excited about it in a way that I never had done before.

Several weeks later Paul opened an opportunity at our house group for people to go forward for ministry.[2] It was the first time this kind of ministry had ever happened in the house group, and I hummed and hawed and wasn't really very sure. But when I went forward I knew that God would meet me, and in such a small gathering, among people whom I knew very well, I could open myself very deeply without fear of being laughed at or closely watched. In going down I was aware of being open to God at a deeper level than ever before. He came to me very gently, and His finger touched the pain. It was agonizing – like having a wound that wasn't healed touched again and again, wave after wave ... while I just lay on the carpet and howled! Though it was very sore, there was peace in it. God was very close, and it didn't worry me that it was happening: at last I felt relief.

That evening in bed I felt myself sleeping in a river of peace such as I had never known in all my life. Waking up in the morning, I could hardly believe the level and depth of peace that was still upon me. During the next week I felt a bit shell-shocked, as if a bomb had gone off at my feet. I was disorientated. The next Wednesday the opportunity was given once more. I knew that God would move again, because the healing was not quite complete. Although I felt a real idiot because all I was doing was lying on the carpet howling, I had to open myself as much as I possibly could to God. On this second occasion when His finger came in again, part of me almost cried to Him, 'I can't take all this pain again – I don't know how long it is going on.' But inwardly I said, 'I don't care how long it's going on. I'm just going to grit my teeth and open myself as wide as I possibly can until it is touched and gone completely.' The waves came, and again it was very painful. Then there was a point when it wasn't sore any more but just numb. I was crying continuously, and as each wave came it seemed to reach a certain depth and go again.

About the fourth or fifth time it came with laughter, and the laughter seemed to open a part deeper than I had ever known before. In a split second the finger of God touched me at that depth, and it was as if a great shout filled the room: 'That's it. You're free!' – and I lay on the carpet and laughed and laughed and laughed. That laughter came into the same depth as the pain had been, replacing it with joy! I have never felt as free as this. After the load I carried about with me for years, the triumph I feel! 'You're free, you're **free**!'

Someone had said to me some years ago, 'God wants to make you a child again inside. What's happened to you? You've changed.' That person didn't know me as a child, but they seemed to have picked up what my spirit was like. As I was lying on the carpet, God said, 'That's it. You're a child again!' It was absolutely wonderful – I would recommend it to anybody!

Joining in the general laughter, I reflected on the inadequacy of so much of Christian ministry. I could have counselled Sue for a hundred years without ever coming on what God ultimately revealed in a few moments of time. Had I touched a sore spot, she would probably have said, 'That's it' – when it was only the beginning of 'it'. Only the Holy Spirit could take her through each stage in His own wonderful way.

A very different kind of report was that offered in retrospect by **Ian L**. A man of many parts, Ian was known both for his musical talent and for his culinary skills in our Greenock coffee shop. The following reflections, supplied

in writing more than two years after the inception of the
new ministry, may lack some of the specific detail of the
impromptu reports he gave from time to time immediately
after ministry. The analysis he offers here is nevertheless
instructive, revealing a wholesome balance in his attitude
to God's ministry in our midst:

> Over the past year or so I have gone forward for
> ministry several times as I have felt led to. Here is
> what I can remember:
> Firstly the type of call which I have responded to:
> (1) to be one of the valiant of the valiant
> (2) letting the wind of the Spirit blow through my
>   life
> (3) tuning into the purposes of God
> (4) knowledge of the fear of the Lord, the
>   awesome, holy One of Israel.
> Certain features have been common to all [occasions]
> as I have been ministered to.
>
> There has been no sense of any physical manifesta-
> tion such as shaking, electricity, burning, liquid love,
> etc. There has been no sense of the audible voice of
> God speaking to me. There has been a general
> awareness of light, but not blinding light. No visions
> or pictures in the mind.
>
> Before going down on the floor I have never felt
> pushed over, nor has there been a sense of the power
> of God forcing me down. Sometimes I have deliber-
> ately stood, trying to see if I am missing something by
> going down too soon, but it's just as if God wants me
> on the floor, and what am I waiting for? – so at my
> own will I let myself go down. This has never been a
> difficulty for me, ever since the first time it happened
> in Beulah, Millport, as I have always felt I am falling
> into Jesus' arms.[3]
>
> Once down on the floor, sometimes there has been a
> period of speaking in tongues, which ceases, and I have
> been left to quieten my mind and just rest in the Lord.

I remember when I responded to the 'fear of the Lord' call, being very grateful for the covering Jesus provided, that I should be able to lie at peace in the presence of Almighty God.

I think the overall result of my going forward for ministry has been a willingness to obey this prompting despite the arguments of my mind; a moving into a more trusting place even though not experiencing any specific vision or other spiritual experience as others have testified to; a stronger conviction of the truth of the teaching of the church; a lovely sense of unity with the leadership and an acceptance of being where the Lord wants me to be, with an openness to change and the patience to wait for the Lord to bring it about.

A namesake, **Ian S**, described the experience he had had the preceding night in Darvel, where Pauline and I had been taking a house meeting at regular intervals. Ian had enjoyed the meetings, but there came an evening in December 1994 that was different:

The sense of God's presence was powerful as Mr Black was relating to us some of the things that had been happening in the church in recent weeks. The meeting was just different. I was the first up for ministry, and Pauline and Mr Black prayed with me. As soon as they touched me, God was so real. It was as if a purple robe came over me, and I went down in spirit. Now I have been going to [charismatic meetings] for many years, and I have been coming to Struthers meetings from time to time as well. But I have never experienced anything like I felt last night. I was out on that carpet for a good half-hour. It was just like being on the operating table. God took away all the hurt, all the failure, and I hope all the sin, and He ministered to me in a really powerful way. He started speaking to me in a way that I have never heard God speak before.

For **Sheila**, a teacher of the deaf, God's operating table meant literal physical healing:[4] In February 1997 she wrote:

> Twice I went out specifically for this purpose in Greenock and was prayed with on one occasion by Owen Martin and on the other by Grace Gault.[5]
>
> I had been troubled over the years with gynaecological problems, which had been worsening and causing me great distress. There was a lot of pain down my right side, and also swelling, which caused much anxiety. My GP treated me with medication, and in January 1996 I went into Inverclyde Royal Hospital for investigation. Under anaesthetic, a laparoscopy was carried out which revealed that one of the problems was adhesions to the bowel.
>
> The consultant said that nothing much could be done. Although she had removed some adhesions under anaesthetic, they would probably grow back. Medication was by now upsetting my system and had to be discontinued.
>
> I went forward for healing because I was so distressed with the situation and knew there was no medical cure. Both times I was prayed for I went down under the power of the Spirit and gave the problem and anxiety over to God.

Although Sheila could not name the date when she was healed, she remembered having told Mrs Gault in the summer of 1996 that she felt much better, and that the old problems had not returned. 'Now, into 1997,' she wrote, 'I realize that God has definitely moved in healing power, and I am well.'

Sheila had gone forward for prayer many times since the new ministry began, and each time, in different ways, had experienced a profound effect. She described a particularly significant instance:

This happened on a recent occasion when the invitation to go forward was given to people who wanted to be warriors for Christ and to be sold out for God and His kingdom. I felt that I had already given much, but wanted to yield totally to God's plans for me.

When Mr Black prayed for me, I went down under the power of the Holy Spirit. I lost consciousness of my whereabouts; it seemed as if my physical body was diminishing, yet my spirit was soaring free. I was going out in my spirit to a very large place of great freedom – free of the constraints of the body, of time and of place. In that spiritual place I felt rather than saw the light of Christ and His power and glory. I felt caught up in that glory, transfused by it and empowered by the strength of Christ.

On coming back to awareness of my surroundings, I felt that something of great significance had happened – something which is still being outworked in my life on a daily basis.

It was always heartening when ministry was sought, as in Sheila's case, not simply in order to receive, but to give. The following report on a visit to Galloway in the south-west of Scotland included a similar element.

In May 1995 **Robert and Agnes Cleary** introduced me to friends in Newton Stewart. We found that an evening meeting had been arranged, attended by a very mixed company of about forty individuals. On our return Bobby (minister of our Gourock church and a personal friend since boyhood) described how the hand of the Lord came down that evening:

As I sat down there came to my mind an old hymn whose chorus went something like this:

The children of the Lord have a right to shout and sing,
For the day is growing bright, and our souls are on the wing.

Bobby's soul was evidently on the wing as he continued:

It was a mixed company indeed, from very different backgrounds. Mr Black spoke and very simply introduced spiritual life to the people. It was lovely to feel divine presence, the powerful presence of the living God in the midst. About three-quarters of the people came out for ministry. The needs were great – and, praise God, the needs were met instantaneously by the coming in of the Spirit of the living God in power.

One instance in particular caused me to rejoice. There came in front of me an older lady who was both extremely tall and as thin as a pole.

Standing there in apprehension, she said, 'You know, I don't want to go down. If I go down, I will never get up!'

I said, 'Don't you worry. If you go down, you will come up!'

And I asked her, as I quite regularly do with people seeking ministry, 'What do you want from the Lord tonight?'

'I've had a burden for years,' she said, 'and I want that burden increased. I want to be a deeper intercessor for the moving of the power of revival in our midst.'

How my heart lifted!

She went down like a feather, and God moved upon her wonderfully. I had the joy of listening in to something of what was happening to that dear lady, and I know that she is rejoicing today.

Another lady, expressing her deep appreciation for the ministry and for the work of God, commented, 'We are bound together to pray for revival.'

I asked Agnes to add her description of what happened on the following morning. Here is her account of how the Christ of Galilee visited a farmhouse in Newton Stewart:

Praise the Lord! He is mighty to save, heal and deliver, and He is just as wonderful in the kitchen as He is in this church.

On the Wednesday morning after we had finished breakfast, the lady with whom we were staying said to Mr Black, 'I would like you to pray for my back and shoulder. For months they have been very painful, and I find it so difficult and wearisome every day with this constant pain.'

Mr Black duly took her aside and prayed for her – and she went down under the mighty hand of God in her own kitchen. Mr Black just stood back, and so did we; I was sitting in a chair further over in the room. And her face was absolutely radiant as she lay there on the floor.

Eventually she got up and said, 'I have no more pain.' She said also, 'It was so glorious down there. The waves of the sea were just rolling over me.'

Mr Black had said to her when he was praying, 'The Lord Jesus is with you, just as He was on the shores of Galilee,' and she had experienced this washing of the water right over her.

She said too, 'I felt a garment touch my hand. It definitely was material.'

And yet we weren't near her at that point. It was lovely to know that she felt the garments of the Master as He touched her and healed her. Praise His wonderful Name.

Not all of those who were ministered to by the Spirit could define exactly what it was He had done. Sometimes their awareness was expressed mainly through imagery, as in the case of **Isabel**. An experienced nurse, Isabel had progressed steadily in her knowledge of God since her conversion some years earlier. She testified to meeting Him deeply on several occasions under the new ministry. One of these happened to be recorded:

As I stood up to pray in our Monday night meeting I had a strange sensation akin to that of being in a tunnel. What was even stranger was that when I began speaking my voice started to echo as if I was indeed in a tunnel. Then in my spirit I saw an open door high up in front of me. Through the door came a very bright shaft of light down towards me. The prayer meeting finished, and I said nothing to anyone. I didn't understand what it meant – if it meant anything at all.

On the following Saturday night, when Mr Black invited people seeking ministry to step out into the aisle I remained in my seat, because I was terrified in case I would land on top of somebody, or hurt the person behind me! Later that week, I told Mr Black that I felt I should have gone out.

Again came the Saturday night. As Mr Black spoke I knew once more that I should go forward. And still I sat, thinking, 'I might fall on top of somebody; I'd better not go.' But while I sat there, as if spoken by an audible voice came the words, *Come ye out and be ye separate*. I stepped out into the aisle, and immediately felt a peace come right over my spirit. From my position near the back of the church I could hear Mr Black's voice in the distance. Then all of a sudden – though I was trying to stay on my feet – it was as if I was getting pushed backwards. I didn't actually feel myself landing on the carpet; I was aware of falling back and into a bright light, but this time instead of coming down towards me the light was all round about me, and I was lying in it. It is very difficult to say what actually happened when I was down there. All I can say with certainty is that I knew the love of God in my being, and I praise His Name for what He has done for me.

To draw again on the medical analogy: it is not necessary that the patient understand all that is happening during surgery. On the contrary, for a major operation it is to be hoped that the anaesthetic has rendered the patient incapable of understanding anything at all! What does matter is that the surgeon knows what he is about. Given the depth of the layers of personality at which God was operating, it is not surprising that His action often went beyond the immediate consciousness or comprehension of the patient. Were this never so, we might well wonder about the genuineness and significance of the experiences.

Notes

1. Janet's own experience of the new ministry is told in the first book of this series, *A View from the Floor* (New Wine Press, 1997).
2. Paul Sharkey, who with his wife Susie runs a weekly meeting in their own home, is active in our Glasgow work. One of our musicians, he is the compiler of some of our original hymns and songs under the title *Born in Fire* (New Dawn Music, 1998).
3. Ian along with his wife and daughter were among the group that came into our fellowship through the house meetings held by Sheila Robertson and Alison Speirs in Millport.
4. Readers of my book *Reflections from David* (New Dawn Books, 1992, © 1991), chapters 17–18, or *Christ the Deliverer* (New Dawn Books, 1991), chapter 7 will remember the wonderful story of the healing of Sheila's back a number of years earlier.
5. For Owen Martin, see chapter 8. For Grace Gault, see chapters 5–6.

Chapter 11

A Day as a Thousand Years, and a Thousand Years as a Day

We are living at a momentous time in the history of the church of Christ, perhaps the most significant time in the lifetime of any of us. Shortly after the beginning of the new ministry in our own circles, at the end of 1994, I had an interesting conversation with **Dr George Marshall** about two prophecies of which he had been reading.[1]

Two Visions

George summarized as follows:

> A Baptist pastor by the name of David Obbard had a vision in 1954 of the valley of dry bones.[2] Ezekiel's original vision unfolds in three stages: in the first the bones come together, in the second the flesh comes upon the bones, and in the third the Spirit of God breathes into the bodies and they become alive. Obbard felt he was told by God what the three stages meant, and it was also indicated to him that each stage would take twenty years. If we take the first to be dated approximately 1954–74, and the second 1974–94, the interesting thing is that the third stage, which is just beginning, is when the Spirit of God

141

breathed into the bodies and there arose a mighty army. And this was the coming of revival.

Now the thing that particularly struck me was that that period ended in 2015, and I had already been reading of a man in Saval, Sutherland, who in 1926 had a dream about a tree.[3] The tree was seen going through various stages of growth, and in 1940 was at its lowest ebb with almost no life in it at all. But by 1960 the process was beginning to be reversed, and the date of 2016 was then given as the point when the tree would be at its most brilliant. What I found very interesting was that the date 2016 ties in very much with the vision that Obbard had, and it seems unlikely that Obbard knew of the earlier vision of this Highland gentleman.

We may note in passing that the hopes of some that Christ will come back at the end of the century will not be fulfilled, if these are accurate visions, and I think they must be treated seriously.

Some Christians, even those interested in biblical prophecy, can feel curiously dwarfed and intimidated by the spectacle that is opened up by visions such as these. The God who can survey the panorama of the years that yet lie hidden in the future must be great beyond our finite comprehension. And there can come the feeling, 'How then can He be bothered with me?'

> *For a thousand years in thy sight are but as yesterday when it is past, and as a watch in the night.*
>
> (Psalm 90:4)

But if a millennium passes away like a flicker before Him, it is also true that a day weighs in His scales like a millennium:

> *One day is with the Lord as a thousand years, and a thousand years as one day* (2 Peter 3:8)

Not only is the great little in His sight: the little is also great. The God who scans the millennia like pages marked 'yesterday', 'today' and 'tomorrow' is the God who records each quiver of thought in a day of any one life. And more than that: His care for us is as boundless as His knowledge.

One testimony brought this out poignantly.

The Healing of Memory

The date was a Saturday night in May 1997, but as he sat listening to the preaching in our Glasgow church **Jack** was transported back to a very different time and situation in his life. Most readers should be able to relate to the incident which had troubled him from time to time in memory.

> About three weeks ago Mr Black was speaking about the tendency, as one grows older, to forget details of recent events, whilst things that happened in the distant past may come clearly and precisely to the forefront of the mind. I have known people for whom not only visual details but even associated smells came back very strongly. My attention was caught by this idea of something from the past coming back very clearly. Mr Black had also spoken that night on the ability of Christ to be in every situation with you, at every point of your life, present or past. Whether he tied the two items together, or whether I even thought through the connection logically, I do not now remember. But it nonetheless has a bearing on what happened as I was sitting listening avidly to everything he was saying.

> One of those situations from away back came to the very front of my mind. The memory was one that would recur from time to time. Though it did not cause deep disturbance or loss of sleep, the emotional pain of it was relived as vividly as if the incident was actually happening all over again.

It had taken place shortly after my return to primary school after having been in hospital for some months. The teacher we had then was perhaps best described as one of the old school. He never sat, but stood rigidly at his high desk on a raised platform. He was one of those endearing teachers whose comprehensive grasp of details such as his pupils' names was revealed in comments such as: 'Boy, take a walk! ... Stupid girl!'

I hesitate to criticize the teaching profession any further! Looking back, one can see the funny side. Nonetheless, the memory brings with it the awareness of pain. I don't know what the catalyst was – whether it was some deficiency in mental arithmetic or in English. But I can remember very vividly the cutting words that were used, words that laid bare, words that opened up, words that broke down and destroyed, words that brought embarrassment to a child in front of his pals – and the inability to explain, as the numbed mind refused to function.

That Saturday night in Glasgow it was as if I was actually there again. I could see very clearly the classroom with its big sash windows, and even the waste paper basket (I suppose it could have been my jotter that was in the middle of it!). I could see distinctly the faces of my schoolmates, and remember their names. And I could see myself – for in a way I was an adult looking in on the situation. I could see the child and could see and feel the hurt, confusion and embarrassment. I could see the teacher.

But then I became aware of something that had never happened before: there was another adult in the room. Turning round to see who it was, I got such a surprise that I said before I realized it, 'What are **You** doing here?'

I knew without a shadow of a doubt that it was Christ. Don't tell me how I knew: I just knew that I knew it was Christ in that classroom.

And Christ looked at me, the adult (I hope this doesn't become confusing, because I get confused by it!), and He did not say anything to me or to anyone at all, so far as I could tell. He just went to the front of the class, and He lifted the child in His arms. It was a very clear picture of Christ taking that child, and the child burying his head in the shoulder of Christ. I don't recall that there were any words spoken. But within myself there was such an assurance of understanding, an assurance that someone knew the child's feeling of confusion and hurt and numbness and inability to explain. And I sensed that all was well: the child was 'safe in the arms of Jesus'. Christ had come in and made the situation whole. Instead of words and feelings that broke down and destroyed, there was a strong sense of things being brought together and not patched over but healed at a very deep level.

Over the next three weeks I have, as it were, conjured up the memory of the original situation. Never has there been that sense of hurt, confusion or disarray. There has always been the assurance that Christ was in that room with the child – and not only was the child healed: the adult was healed as well.

Coming through Jack's story is the constant flow of the love of God. The great appeal of such a testimony is the analysis of what happens in the heart. It is not just a case of, 'Well, I went down under the power and it was wonderful, and I got up, and life has changed.' Instead it goes deeply into the kind of specific and intimate detail that brings the reality home to us.

The Bible Code

In the same month that Jack's healing took place, the *Daily Mail* published a series of excerpts from a book about to be released on what was described as 'the Bible

Code'. Written by a journalist Drosnin, the book created something of a sensation.[4] Its kernel was a statistical experiment, originally published in a reputable scientific journal, that suggested that the writer of the Pentateuch had encoded within the text details of men yet unborn. The scale of the code was such that it could have been neither devised nor uncovered by a mind of less than computer-like ability.

Reactions both in and out of Christian circles were predictably divided. Arguments raged in print and over the Internet between those qualified and some less qualified to discuss the technical aspects. Some Christians felt the whole idea so alien to their conception of God's ways that they did not give it serious consideration. Others were awed and moved by the possibility that details of the march of history and even one's own puny life might be enshrined in a text that had been extant for centuries, encoded in the very book that had lain around one's house in some version or other, for as far back as memory went.

I myself was cautiously impressed. No Christian should have trouble accepting the fact that the Bible is in a straightforward way predictive. In the Old Testament you find, for example, many predictions about the coming of Christ. Any difficulty in the concept of a Bible Code need not lie in its predictive aspect. Thinking of the claims made for the Code, I suddenly realized that, if they were true, the mind which planned this could not be a finite mind. No human being, no computer, no mechanical means that we could have instituted, could have done it. The history of the whole world (it seemed) might well be encoded in that work. Think of it: your every action encoded, written as with an iron pen on rock: absolutely encoded and known from the beginning.[5]

I do not want, nor am I equipped, to pursue the technical side of the subject.[6] What I want to get to is the spiritual side: the intense concentration on individual lives. There is a connecting link with what Jack had to say. It has brought to mind something I have always found quite staggering – something that at a merely intellectual level would be difficult to grasp or to believe. The world's population is vast, numbering many millions. Through the ages there have been hundreds of millions of people alive. Any one life has millions of happenings: thoughts, words, deeds, experiences. And here suddenly the Lord Jesus comes to a man on earth and goes back with that man over the years and decades, and He stands with him in an embarrassing situation that to everyone but that man was of no significance whatever – but it has an effect on that man's spiritual life. Jesus goes right back to that very scene. And is He doing that in millions of lives at the same time? – because we all have a backlog of experience to be straightened out and sorted.

I suddenly feel I am in the presence of an infinite intelligence – and it is the same intelligence that some think is behind the Bible Code, if such a thing exists. It is the infinite God. It has a double effect on you. It makes you feel terribly small, as the fine dust in the balance. And it makes you feel tremendously significant in the eyes of Jesus, that He should have come in and gone down that road with Jack, and stood in that room, decades back, and healed a memory. Such is the love of Jesus, the omnipotence and omniscience of Jesus, the all-lovingness of our God.

Notes

1. George Marshall is featured in my *Christ the Deliverer* (New Dawn Books, 1991), where the story is told of his healing from manic depression. God has greatly blessed George's work as a scientist. As research director for a bio-medical firm, he has collected a steadily growing list of national prizes, including a SMART award, two Millennium Product awards and a regional John Logie Baird award.
2. Ezekiel 37:1–14. For Obbard's vision, see Dave Roberts, *The 'Toronto' Blessing* (Kingsway Publications, 1994), pp. 27–8).
3. In Murdoch Campbell, *Gleanings of Highland Harvest* (Christian Focus Publications, 1st impression 1953; new, enlarged edition 1957), p. 123.
4. Michael Drosnin, *The Bible Code* (Weidenfeld & Nicolson, 1997; Orion Paperback edition published by arrangement with Simon & Schuster Inc., 1997).

5. The suggestion was not that all things were ordained in such a way that they were unalterable, but that the Code revealed at times the detail of possibilities where the situation could go one way or the other.

6. At the time of writing the best source for both the technical aspects and current status of the Bible Code is, so far as I am aware, Randall Ingermanson, *Who Wrote the Bible Code? A Physicist Exposes the Myths* (California: Waterbrook, 1997). The reader will appreciate that we are not here concerned with whether claims made for the Code are true. What is important for our immediate purpose is the concept of a God whose infinite knowledge, power and loving interest in the lives of His creatures could in principle be revealed in such a form.

Chapter 12

A Gleam From the North

'**A glowing beacon**'. The *Daily Mail* headline with its accompanying photograph was arresting. The article that it introduced was of more than ordinary interest – for it concerned a good friend of ours and described how his congregation on the north coast had bucked the national trend:[1]

It may be considered a distant outpost by most of Scotland, but Thurso in Caithness has earned the label of the most God-fearing town in the nation.

Despite experiencing a drop in population, the town has notched up the double Kirk firsts of fastest-growing congregation and highest attendance rate in Scotland.

The Rev Kenneth Borthwick's charge – St Peter's and St Andrews – emerged as a flourishing beacon in a Church of Scotland report.

At the imposing town-centre kirk, with its landmark clock tower, eight out of ten members attend every Sunday against an average of 30 per cent across the country.

Many of them have also been converted to the controversial 'Toronto Blessing' phenomenon, where believers tremble, laugh and cry out. But where other kirks have experienced a fall in attendance when evangelical forms of worship have been introduced,

Mr Borthwick has seen congregations double since his arrival in 1989.

Father-of-two Mr Borthwick retains traditional Sunday morning services but introduced aspects of the blessing to his evening services in 1994. The Glasgow-born minister is sure it has led to the explosive growth. He said: 'I believe that this is God's way of refreshing the spirits of churchgoers.

'I realise that some people do not accept this interpretation, but I have seen for myself people shaking and literally falling under the influence of this power.'

The article, published in May 1997, went on to cite the opposite situation in another part of the north, where church attendance was particularly poor. It was suggested by one of the sources quoted that historical and cultural factors might explain the different attendance rates. Without dismissing historical and cultural influences as irrelevant, let us nevertheless hear what the **Rev. Kenny Borthwick**, minister of the church in Thurso, has to say about the specific and miraculous action of God in that place.

We had known Kenny ever since the days when as a divinity student he used to drop into our Knightswood church in Glasgow. It was at that time that he had received his baptism in the Spirit. About two weeks after the article appeared in the *Daily Mail*, he visited our Saturday night meeting while down for the General Assembly of the Church of Scotland.

At the time of Kenny's visit, I was awaiting the publication of the first book of this series, *A View from the Floor*. Knowing that Kenny himself was very open to the moving of the Spirit, and that in recent times he had known much of the blessing of God, I mentioned the forthcoming book when introducing him anew to the company; an unexpected rejoinder came in the course of his report. Kenny's own story is well worth telling, and he has been kind enough to allow us to include here what he told us of the moving of God in his own life and on the people of Thurso.

A 'Toronto' blessing in Edinburgh

Mr Black made reference to the fact that I should be at the Assembly tonight but chose to be here instead. That reminds me of how this began back in October 1994, when my people in Thurso thought I was in Edinburgh at the Church offices, and in fact I was at a meeting about the Toronto blessing.

The first I had ever heard about this move of God was from the manse window cleaner. When he told me about some of the manifestations, there was an immediate anger within me at the very idea that he could think this was God.

I thought, 'This is not God.'

At the same time something leapt within me with the very definite assurance, 'This is God!'

I decided that along with one of my elders and another member of the congregation I would go to a Church of Scotland meeting in Edinburgh where two of the Toronto pastors would be speaking. I cannot tell you how out of place I felt at the first meeting. I felt totally and utterly judgmental of everything that was going on. Having stood next to some of the ministry team while waiting to register for this conference, I have to tell you I did not like them: it's as simple as that. I did not like these people. As the meeting progressed, I did not like the manifestations.

It came to the preaching, and that was quite wonderful. I was impressed by the humility of the person speaking, and by the fact that over in Toronto they didn't know why this had happened. They were not making any pretensions to be especially holy. They did not say they had been praying for this. Something very definitely started to come home to me – because a few months before, in my own prayer time, God had said to me, 'There's going to be a new move in the land, and the marks of it are going to be the revelation of the Father's heart and the Father's kiss.' And after about an hour of this meeting, the preacher stood up and said, 'Don't be put off by the manifestations. This move of God is about the revelation of the Father's heart. It's about the Father's kiss for His children. So many Christians really don't know that God loves them.'

By the end of the meeting, however, I was still feeling judgmental. I had decided I was going home – and this puts the fear of God into me: how much I might have missed. I was intending to go home and not wait for prayer. But then all of a sudden I suppose something of the Scotsman in me thought, 'Well, if God's got anything for me I want it.' My elder, who's from Aberdeen, felt the same, only more so! And so did the other fellow, who was from the Borders. Consequently the three of us, having decided we weren't going forward for prayer ... went forward for prayer.

I saw my elder and my other friend being prayed for: down they went.

I thought, 'I know what's going to happen to me: nothing!' Back in the 1970s I had been prayed for in this way in several places; the only time I went down was when I was pushed over.

I stood there, saying to God, 'Lord, You know how hard I'm finding this. I feel so judgmental, so critical towards these people. I know this is wrong, but I cannot change this attitude. I can only confess it, and say to You, if anything shows that I need the blessing of God it's the hardness in my heart towards these people.'

Somebody came towards me, and simply said, 'What's your name?'

I said, 'Kenny.'

He did not lay a hand on me – or perhaps lightly touched my finger-tips. All he said was, 'Lord, bless Kenny.'

And I was hit by the most incredible force – literally lifted off my feet and flung back, presumably into arms that were waiting for me. I lay there on the floor, with the grace, the love and the power of God sweeping through me for about forty-five minutes. It was as though I could see the golden glory of God, and there was my life in that glory, with my sins and everything that needed forgiven and changed. And then, as it were, the camera drew back, and I could see that God was higher and deeper and wider than I had ever perceived. The camera drew back, and drew back – and I began to see how big God was. And there was I with my needs and my sin in the heart of it all, for His love and mercy to change.

Over the course of the next few days I spent a lot of time admiring the ceiling.

This news about the book *A View from the Floor* is very interesting, because I remember writing to a publisher suggesting I would like to write a book about this, and the response was, 'Well, no, we don't want one from you, because there's another man from Scotland writing a book called *Views from the Floor*. So this must be the one!

Having imparted this intriguing piece of information, Kenny continued the account of his own 'view from the floor':

That went on for about three days. I spent so much time on the floor in the presence of God that I missed almost everything that was being said in the services. That didn't bother me; it's better to meet with God.

Return to Thurso
At the end of the three days we went back home to Thurso. The church is a very traditional one, and the three of us had received so much that we wanted to

give it away. We had no inkling at all that God would do what He did. There was no word on it, no great faith in our hearts. We simply shared our experience after an evening service, and said, 'If anyone wants to stay behind, please do.' About twenty or thirty stayed behind that night. We started to sing, and I say 'sing' because it wasn't worship; we were simply singing, and God told me this.

He said, 'You're only singing because you're afraid if you pray nothing will happen.' And that was true.

He said, 'Would you stop singing and just pray for the people?'

So we stopped singing, and folk came forward. There was no great feeling of power, no great rush, no great faith. But within five minutes, about twenty-five of the thirty people were flat on their backs, just drinking in the blessing of God.

Stages of blessing

To describe this as briefly as possible, over the course of the next months people were renewed. That was the first stage: the **renewing of the people of God**.

Basically the work has progressed through hearing the word of the Lord. At a certain stage He said to us, **'Get ready for the firstfruits.'** What happened on the following Sunday was unprecedented. Two outsiders had come into our evening service. During the course of the service, before ministry time, one of them went crashing out forward in front of her seat, and the other went *splat!* against the wall at the back. After the service was over I went up to the first of them; she had never been in church before in her life.

I said to her, 'What did you feel?'

She had never read her Bible, and yet she said, 'I felt such love, such joy, such peace.' Then I introduced her to a couple whom she knew in the church and said, 'Speak to this couple, and they'll tell you the source of that.'

The next day I went to see the one who had gone *splat!* against the wall, and when I walked through the door with one of the lady leaders from the church, she handed me over a pendulum. She had been into white witchcraft. She said that when she had gone *splat!* against the wall God had spoken into her heart and said, 'If you want My Son, you cannot go on doing this.'

It makes being a minister considerably easier when God comes!

I think of somebody else whom I met on the first day of 1996.

He said, 'The Lord's told me 1996 is going to be the year for me to come to Him.'

I said, 'Well, you better not leave it too long. You might get knocked down by a bus.'

The last Sunday of 1996 he was in the bookie's. He was a notorious gambler. People thought he worked in the bookie's, because for fifteen years since coming to Thurso he was in there every day: he just took his packed lunch and spent the whole day there.

On that last Sunday of the year God spoke to him in the bookie's and said, 'What are you doing following horses when you could be following Jesus Christ?' That Sunday he walked out of the bookie's into the church, and in the afternoon he was saved.

So that was the next phase, and it came through hearing the word of the Lord, 'Get ready for the firstfruits.'

To move on very quickly, there came a point where God seemed to say: 'It's time for the **daughters of Zion** to arise.'

The Church of Scotland is not like Struthers, and certainly not in our congregation, where women were consigned to making the tea. God came and said that He was not happy with that: it was time for the daughters of Zion to arise. He said that there were Christian marriages where the husbands were oppressing their wives, perhaps because the wives' gifting outshone the husbands'. God was not pleased with that: it was time for the daughters of Zion to arise. And no sooner had He said that than women started to come into ministry, particularly in the realm of prayer and prophecy. And I tell you, there are one or two in Thurso who pray so powerfully that I am sincerely glad I am not the devil.

That was the next phase.

Let me tell you what I think God has been saying just lately to us. I think He has been saying that there is a time to build stronger foundations. What He means by that is simply obedience to the word of the Lord: **holiness**. From the time I first visited Struthers about twenty years ago, it has always been a mark of this church. Let me tell you, we've got nothing like this. We in Thurso are the fastest-growing congregation in the Church of Scotland, but the quality of spiritual life here in Struthers is just wonderful. The mark of this place always has been the theme of death to self and holiness, and I believe that's why God blesses.

God said to us, 'That's what I want to take you into: holiness,' into the place of the fear of the Lord, where we actually fear sinning against Him.

On a recent visit to Toronto, in one of the meetings when I was lying on the floor myself, I felt that God came and gave me a picture of an approaching storm. It was black and terrifying. Most people had heeded the warning, and the roads were clear. But two cars that had not heeded the warning were engulfed by the storm. And God seemed to say to me, 'There's always somebody that ignores the warning. It's time for the church to realize that the days of Ananias and Sapphira are coming back.'

The kindness of the Lord

So I think that is the next phase for us, that He wants His people to be a holy people. But we must hold things in perspective. We are to behold the kindness and the severity of the Lord. I think the thing that has come out for me over these last few years has been God's amazing kindness, amazing mercy. He knows us absolutely, He knows us through and through. We have seen so many people's burdens being lifted at Calvary. When new people started to come, one of the things that God said to us was, 'They are not going to be the sort of people that many churches would hold up with pride as their converts. They are going to be off-the-wall, a wee bit weird, not the sort of folk whose lives are all together.'

And so it has proved to be. I can think of folk in our church now that come out of a background of abuse, alcoholism or drug addiction. That wasn't the case up until two years ago. But I would not have missed getting to know them for the world, seeing what God has done in them: they have learned to receive the love of God, and they have learned to give it away even to me. So God has come in kindness.

One more story from Toronto sums up that side of it. There was one lady who got up and stood at the microphone, gently shaking. She said, 'You know, I've been so critical of this. As I've watched this, I have seen folk doing things, and I was sure they could control it.' And she said, trembling, 'Now I know you can't!'

She continued, 'There are only two people whom I have ever felt were happy in my presence – my mother and my father – and they both died last year. When I was sitting there, God came to me and said, "I am happy to be in your presence." Not, "I am happy to have you in My presence," but "I am happy to be in your presence."' The kindness of the Lord!

I am very, very grateful for all that God has done.

Mr Black was speaking about how God doesn't want your plans or your gifting; He just wants your death. Similarly when David wanted to build a house for the Lord, God said to him, 'I don't want you to build a house for Me; I want to build a house for you.' I was reminded of this when during one of the prayer times in Toronto God came to me and said, 'I know all that you want to do for me in Thurso. But I don't want any of that. This is what I want to do for you and for My glory.'

I look forward to what the Lord might yet do.

These have been a wonderful few years, marked by the fulfilment of revelation. One of the pastors from Toronto came and took a meeting in our congregation. He was a lovely, gentle sort of person; I think he was Irish originally, and had only been in Canada for three years. He seemed to fit in well with the northern temperament.

Before he went he said, 'Kenny, I feel strongly that within the Church of Scotland God is going to make this congregation a lighthouse. Other people are going to look at it and ask, "Why is this happening?"'

Interestingly, the headline in the *Daily Mail* was, 'A glowing beacon'. I think that is the Lord coming to be faithful to His word. Though I wouldn't compare what we've got with what's happening in Struthers, neither would I have missed it for the world. It has been wonderful.

Comparisons are perhaps best avoided. What God has done in Thurso I reckon is very wonderful indeed. Kenny continues:

The attendance has grown from one hundred to two hundred. We have people who have never been inside church in their lives. Children are starting to come to know the Lord, which has not happened before – and this will be my last story.

One little six-year-old boy was very serious when he went home one day from a Scouts service.

'What's the matter?' asked his mum.

He said, 'I'm just thinking about what Kenny was saying.'

Still serious, he said to his mum, 'I'm just going through to my room for a minute.'

When he came back he said, 'Mum, can I tell you something? Do you promise you'll not laugh?'

'I promise I'll not laugh.'

'Do you promise you'll not tell my big sister?'

'I promise I'll not tell your big sister.'

'Mum, I asked Jesus into my life.'

'Why did you do that?'

'Well, Kenny said in the church today at the Scouts service, if even just one of you goes home and asks Jesus into your life ... Mum, I've been thinking a long time about that' (says this six-year-old). 'The time has just never been right. But today the time was right. Mum, before I asked Jesus into my life, I didn't feel good "in here". When I asked Him in, I had this wonderful feeling.'

That's what I believe it's about. It's about folk feeling the love of God. I used to be in Orkney, known for the shortest scheduled flight in the world, from Westray to Papa Westray. You are just up and then you're down again. But as a minister, certainly in the Church of Scotland, I think the longest spiritual journey in the world for many people is the time it takes the love of God to get from the head to the heart. And I think that process has been speeded up through this blessing. The felt love of God is the answer to ninety-nine per cent of people's problems: just to feel God's love.

Kenny ended with a word of advice to his audience:

Don't be like what I nearly was in Edinburgh. Had I followed my decision to go out of the church doors and go home, I believe before God that none of this would have happened. Don't play fast and loose with the blessing of God. If you feel a need, then make sure when it comes to the ministry time that you come. Don't let your sins keep you away. He knew my sinful heart, the judgmentalism, the criticism. But I think if you are prepared to be totally honest before God (this is a principle I learned from Mr Black), then He will meet you, whatever your need, and whatever state you come in.

So thanks for listening, and thanks for this church too. I'm not going to praise Mr Black, but I feel so refreshed through seeing him. It's been five years since I've been down here, and it's lovely to see him and to be in such worship. Five years ago I said, 'I don't know anywhere like this in Scotland, where the stream of worship is so deep and the presence of God so real.' There may be other places that are busier, there may be other places that in some senses are livelier. But I know of none where the stream of God is so deep. And I hope that some of you will come and stand in it, or lie down in it, get into it, tonight.

We felt the lovely touch of the Holy Spirit as Kenny spoke of the wondrous, drawing love of Christ and His desire to bless the sons of men. I noted too what Kenny had to say of the storm and the possible danger. It reminded me of something my daughter Mary had said at the opening of our new church building in Cumbernauld, that the devil will fight over the salvation of a soul, and he will fight over a baptism in the Holy Spirit, but the fight that he puts up on these fronts is very little, compared to the fight that he puts up against a person who is making that full, total commitment to go into the place of holiness. I have believed for many years that the key is holiness unto the Lord and death to the carnal nature. I was very encouraged by Kenny's attitude in the matter.

By Their Fruits You Shall Know Them

Meanwhile the Church of Scotland had decided to 'monitor' the effects of the so-called Toronto Blessing. A measure of antagonism reared its head also with the publication of a booklet prepared by a minister of the same denomination. Though aware that not all were happy with the reports emanating from Thurso, Kenny nevertheless welcomed the decision to monitor what was going on; he had reason to expect that the good fruit in his parish would become apparent. He brought us up to date with events in and beyond his own congregation when he visited us again in October 1997:

Physical healing

I went home after my last visit to the story of a marvellous and miraculous healing that had happened while I was away. A retired nurse in our congregation had been visiting her daughter in the Glasgow suburb of Bearsden and was taken into hospital with a severe liver problem. During the course of her illness the liver swelled to give the impression of a full-term pregnancy; she was very blown out indeed, and that is medically a bad sign. Eventually her daughter phoned the church in Thurso and asked us to pray. Since I was away at the time, my wife Morag took the message, and prayer was made at the church services.

What happened next was astonishing. The whole family thought that the lady was dying: doctors had more or less alerted them to this outcome. Meanwhile she had been sent home from the hospital. While lying in bed in her daughter's home, she heard in her ears the song, 'Be still and know that I am God.' When it came to the verse, 'I am the Lord that healeth thee,' the music got louder and louder, and somehow she felt she had to get out of bed. She went downstairs, and her daughters chorused, 'Mum, what are you doing?'

She said, 'Oh, you'll not understand. But do you know this song?' and sitting down at the piano she started to play the song.

Her daughters were none the wiser, and she went back up to bed. During the early hours of the following morning, she awakened to what she describes as a sound of electricity, and accompanying this sound she felt as though a very tight black silk sheet had been pulled through her body. The sensation of something tight or constricting settled over the region of her liver for quite a while and then went right through her body as though something was being drawn out. And she heard in her ears the promise, 'In two days' time you will be healed.'

The next day she felt acutely ill. But faith had been born in her heart, and she said to her daughters, 'It's all right. I'm going to be healed,' and she told them how God had promised her that on the following day there would be a sign confirming her healing.

Without going into personal detail, suffice it to say that on the second day there was a physiological sign that as a nurse she recognized was completely imposs-ible. Without a shadow of a doubt she was healed, and all the symptoms, bar some mild remains of jaundiced colouring, were totally and utterly gone on the second day.

She went to one of the top consultants in the country. All the consultant said was, 'No, this is not possible; this can't happen.' Our friend described some details, and the consultant just shook her head and said, 'No, that can't have happened to you.' The lady says that she lacked the courage then to say it was the Lord. But since then her written testimony has circulated widely. I give praise to God for that.

The story of her healing was awaiting me when I returned. The good things happen when I'm away! Maybe there's something in that, you know – it's very easy in a Church of Scotland set-up for a congrega-tion to look solely to the minister. Maybe that's why the best things happen when I'm away!

Inner healing

That was a case of physical healing. Let me tell you a case of inner healing, affecting myself. This is no reflection on my parents at all – I had a brilliant childhood, with parents as perfect as any parents can be. But from the age of 13 there was a vulnerability in my life that I never shared with a single living soul until I met Morag, who is now my wife. Her understanding and her love brought a measure of healing with regard to that inner vulnerability. But about six or eight weeks ago in my own private prayer time, God seemed to say to me very distinctly, 'Do you know that for you to be really free of this there needs to be somebody else that knows other than your wife?' I said, 'Yes, Lord,' because I had come to that very conviction. So I knew this was coming, but I did not know in what form.

At the end of our evening service two or three Sundays ago, during the time of ministry an elder's wife came forward and started to pray with me. Instantly I knew that she was zeroing in on this vulnerability. A word of knowledge was given in terms of a picture, and I could feel a sort of trembling, a mixture of feelings. On the one hand, 'Oh, no – is that where we're going? Not tonight. I didn't think it would be tonight.' And yet mixed with that there was a joy, because I knew that freedom was in the air, freedom had been promised, freedom was coming. And in the course of minutes a burden of some 27 years was utterly lifted. Although there are certain facts that cannot be altered, these no longer have any hold on me whatsoever. It is a marvellous demonstration of God's might that He can bring instant release from something so longstanding. I really believe that if He could do that for me He can do anything for anyone: that's how deep the need was, and that is the conviction with which the healing has left me.

Dry bones live

On the wider scale, the work has been going on. We are maybe not seeing quite so much trembling and shaking and falling in the time of personal ministry. But I believe that there is a move of God amongst the 'dry bones' – the people who have been on the outskirts of the church for years, or even more recently. God is really beginning to draw them. Mr Black used to say that when told early in his ministry that he must get rid of the dead wood, his reply was, 'But it's up to me to make something of the dead wood as well.' I have seen these folk round about the edges and wondered if they would ever come to the Lord. One of them whose family has been connected for years was standing outside the church a couple of Sundays ago, and as my wife spoke to him he had tears in his eyes. After about 20 minutes, since it was lunchtime, Morag said, 'Well, I'd better stop speaking to you now,' and he clung on to her and said, 'Oh, no, please don't stop speaking.' That's the sort of thing that's happening now: folk on the outskirts who don't know the Lord but are beginning to be drawn.

That same Sunday in the evening, somebody with a bit of a history of notoriety in the town of Thurso came in before the service had even started, sidled up to me and said, 'Kenny, is it really true that God can forgive you for all your sin? I've done such bad things. Is it really true that God can forgive you for all your sin?'

So we looked up 1 John 9 together, '*If we confess our sins, God is faithful and just to forgive us our sins and to cleanse us from all unrighteousness.*' We just focused on that little word 'all'. The teachability of folk on the verge is lovely – he just said, 'Oh, I see! Great, great! Thanks, Kenny,' and away he went quite happy.

Afterwards I asked him, 'Do you want to speak to me any more about this?'

'No, no,' he said. 'What you said earlier was just right. That's great, that's great.'

That's the sort of thing that's happening now – folk just beginning to feel their way towards the Lord.

Laughter

But some of the more dramatic manifestations are still going on. I think of a young single mum who joined the church a couple of Sundays ago. She has a most unfortunate history in terms of abuse within her family, and has had a miserable life in many ways. She joined the church in the morning, and in the evening she came forward for prayer. And she collapsed on the floor, an absolutely helpless heap of laughter.

Now at the beginning of all of this it was the laughter that folk really had difficulty with. I had a bit of difficulty with it too, until I thought, 'Well, it's a bit odd, isn't it, that we think that weeping can be from the Lord but laughter can't?' – as though the Lord never gives joy.

God really rebuked me over this when He said, 'If you don't like the sound of laughter you better get used to it quick.'

And then He said to me, 'Do you realize that some folk have never laughed? Some folk have never laughed with real joy.'

I wouldn't be surprised if that was the case for this young woman. It was so lovely to see her filled to overflowing with a joy that she couldn't contain. And, you know, some folk criticize that. I know that folk who are great students of revival (especially the Lewis revival) ask, 'How does that square with what we've seen and known?'

For their benefit, I can remember a story coming out of the Lewis revival. It concerns a well-known preacher (still active) who came out of that revival. Her father had said, 'I would give anything to be able to go out and stand in the garden and proclaim to all the world, 'I'm clean – clean – clean.' Now when this young girl who collapsed in a heap of laughter on the floor of the church in Thurso came up again, do you know what she said?

'I feel so clean – I feel so clean – I feel so clean!'

Opponents of what God is now wanting to do in the way that He's doing it need to hear testimonies like that. It was wonderful to see. I have heard Rodney Howard Browne, who is often vilified, preach powerfully on two occasions on video. When asked by a critic, 'Why do folk fall down? Why do folk laugh?' he simply replied, 'Maybe your mother never told you, folk laugh when they're happy, and folk fall down when they can't stand up!'

Sometimes I wonder why we need any more explanation than that!

The soul of Scotland

As recently as last Wednesday night God laid on my heart something wider than Thurso. I bless God for what's happening in Thurso, but, you know, it's Scotland that I care about, really – I do want to see the heart of this nation revived. I felt very strongly that God laid a picture and a revelation within my heart for this land. He seemed to say to me that the soul of Scotland was lion-shaped. That speaks of something to do with fierceness, something to do with defiance that Scotland has shown time and time again for the Lord in days past. And He seemed to say that this lion's soul was a reflection of something of Christ Himself, the Lion of the tribe of Judah. And then He went on to say to me this: 'You know, it's great what's happening in Brownsville, what's happening in Toronto, what's happening in Sunderland' – and may I say at this stage that I believe all of these are works of God. But I think God said to me, as a warning to me or to any of those in the Church of Scotland who are thirsty and hungry to see the heart of the nation revived: 'You don't want to try and tame the soul of

Scotland to jump through Sunderland hoops, or to sit
on Toronto stools, or to roll on Brownsville barrels.
There is something unique about the soul of Scotland
that has arisen in the past. It is a reflection of
something of the heart of the Lion of the tribe
of Judah.' And I think that is what we need to see
revived. I have not got all of it from the Lord yet. But
I think there are certain aspects, as follows.

Number one is the **preaching of the word of God**.
Please accept that I am not being critical but merely
factual. With some of the videos that come out of
these renewal centres, it's as though if someone stands
and shakes their head and does something odd they'll
be listened to: but where is anyone just opening up the
word of God and preaching it? In the past Scotland
has stood for the word of God, and specifically for
holiness and for the commandments of God and His
righteousness. When Scotland is revived that is something we are going to contribute to world-wide
revival: a recall to righteousness and the commandments of God and the word of God.

Connected with this is the second aspect: a **recall to
Christ as King**. I wrote something for a Church of
Scotland Renewal network not long ago, an article
called 'The Sound of Distant Knocking?' In it I asked
how it is possible to go into many evangelical
churches in the Church of Scotland, hear wonderful
expository sermons that do seem to go through the
word – but never hear mention of Christ. I pointed
out that you can go into many Renewal services and
hear much about renewal, much about prophecy
and where God is going and what He is going to do
– but you'll not hear much of Christ Himself. And
you know, it has always been precious to me that
Struthers has always been Christ-centred. I have never
been left in any doubt that this is not simply a
movement, though God has blessed it; it is something
that centres on Christ Himself. And I do just wonder

if even in Renewal circles there is maybe the sound of distant knocking – Christ knocking on the door of His own Church as He did in Revelation 3:20, saying, 'If anyone hears me and opens the door, I really will come in'?

Another thing that Scotland has stood for in the past has been the good old-fashioned doctrine of **Providence and fear of the Lord**. It does worry me that sometimes Renewal almost sounds as though it is harnessing God! 'God is going to do this here, and then we're expecting Him to do that.' It's as though we've got God tied up by our prophecies. God is bigger than our prophecies. He is bigger than our understanding of Him. And I think one of the things Scotland can contribute towards all that God is doing is this doctrine of the fear of the Lord and Providence, that knows what it is to bow before Him and say, 'Thy will be done.'

So that is where we are at the moment, and I hope that some of it will tie in with what maybe you are sensing here in your own midst.

A stillness of God's presence had come earlier as Kenny was speaking, and my spirit answered very strongly to what he was saying now. God does His own thing in His own place, and we are not expected to be pale copies one of another. When He moves in power in Scotland, it will have its own flavour: of that I am persuaded.

Visions from God

Nearly a year and a half passed, and then one day I received a letter from a friend who had heard Kenny speaking about certain new visions he had received. My friend had written in some detail, and I in my turn was impressed. Hoping to use his information both in our own church circles and in a forthcoming UCB broadcast, I phoned Kenny to ask his permission. We chatted things through; he was very pleased to allow me to use these details, but after I had indicated to him that he was very welcome to come and preach, he phoned back to say that he had felt a quickening and would in fact like to share what he had received, which I invited him to do at our Saturday night meeting. He came in March 1999 and described first of all the further unfolding of the vision of the lion and its implications. Here is what he told us:

> In a way I gave myself an invitation, but I felt very strongly I was to be here and share this with you: there was just that sense of quickening. I'm not one who sees visions, or whatever we may care to call them, very frequently. As John Wimber says of his operation in the gift of knowledge, I can't turn it on and I can't turn it off. I can only make the most of what I'm given: to share what I believe God has shown concerning his purposes for this land. I feel quite vulnerable doing that, because there's no way that I can prove to you that this is from God, so all I can ask you to do is to submit it to the witness of the Spirit within your own hearts.

The sleeping lion

About a year and a half ago when I was praying I believe that the Lord gave me a vision of the soul of Scotland, and explained to me that every nation had its own particular soul. The soul of Scotland was lion-shaped. He showed me a picture of a sleeping stone lion, bound in chains. Christ Himself was sitting beside it, waiting for the lion to awaken and arise. And He said, 'You see, once the soul of Scotland was fierce and warrior-like for Me.'

I have found that when something comes from God, you can't change it. Nothing that I could do or pray could alter that picture. Much as I might have wanted to see it differently, much as I might have wanted to see this stone lion unbound, coming to life and standing on its feet, nothing could make that picture change. I find that is the mark of something that comes from God.

One of the first times that God gave me a vision, it was concerning a little girl in Stronsay, Orkney, where I was first a minister. My wife and I had just been speaking to her in the island shop and asked her, 'Will we see you at the young folk's group tomorrow night?'

'Yes,' she said. She had just been converted only a couple of weeks before.

She stepped outside the shop and was hit by a car.

I remember going with the island doctor to the airstrip from which she was flown off, and then going back home and praying. This was one of the first pictures God ever gave me. I saw this wee girl sleeping on the top part of an hourglass. The sand was running out, and ever so gently and with a look of real peace in her face she slipped through the neck of the hourglass and continued to sleep down below. And I knew what that meant: she was going to die. Everything in me wanted to pray against it, and everything in me tried to imagine this wee girl up in the top part of the hourglass, but I just couldn't do it – because when something is from God, nothing can alter it. And the picture of the stone lion came with the same forcefulness. It was unalterable fact that the soul of Scotland was sleeping and bound in chains.

The lion awakes

But just about a month ago when I was praying again for the land, all of a sudden and without any warning the picture changed. The lion was up on its feet. It was looking very weary and very tired, and it didn't even know it was a lion. But it was up on its feet, unchained. And there's a part of this I don't understand. I don't really know what has happened, except that in the spiritual realm something has shifted concerning this nation, and it has been brought about through the intercession of God's people. I am absolutely convinced of that. Perhaps we thought that we would just pray and pray and pray, and nothing would ever change. God has shown me that something has changed, and I think that what has changed is an apathy and a tiredness and a weariness upon the hearts of God's people. The Bible says that hope deferred makes the heart sick, and some of us have waited many decades for revival and grown weary. I think the lion being up on its feet signifies that through the intercession of the people of God the chains of weariness and tiredness and being worn out spiritually have actually been broken.

You know, Satan loves to wear us out. It's an amazing thing: it is a law of the kingdom of darkness that it takes what is good and causes something not good to happen through it. The kingdom of darkness takes the law of God that is good and through the law of God causes sin to arise within our hearts and spring to life, as Paul says in Romans 7. I think that Satan has been wearing out the people of God by getting the church to try this and that scheme to bring about church growth or revival. And we, the people of God, with our desire to see God move and be glorified, swallow the bait hook, line and sinker, and try one thing after another until God's people eventually get worn out.

God gave me a picture during our evening service not long ago. There appeared a horse-drawn carriage coming right through the service. It was a beautiful-looking carriage, and God said to me, 'Will you remember that the finest of carriages can conceal the cruellest of men?' (I feel the anointing of God on that, so this is maybe for some of us that are worn out.) As the carriage came past I looked in, and what I saw was a sort of Dracula-type figure – you know, Dracula by folklore sucks blood and takes away people's life and strength. I saw him riding through the church, whipping things up almost to a frenzy. Then the impression was that he was riding out through our church and through the land trying to whip the people of God up to more and more activity – which seems like a good idea but was just wearing out the people of God. A big part of the born-again, even Spirit-filled, church has become worn out. And I think that something has shifted with regard to that, and what the people of God are going to find is a new awareness that God is going to do something big, a restoration of faith and hope that we're soon going to see a day of God's power.

So I saw this lion arising, and that represents the soul of Scotland just beginning to arise. But the soul of Scotland is still very shaky on its feet, very tired, very weary, and isn't yet aware of its own identity as a lion.

The strengthening of the lion

And what I saw was that this lion began to wander into different churches. In one church, which has a reputation for being alive, when the congregation saw a lion coming in they cleared out! (Well, you would!) It reminds me of a cartoon in the *Herald* in which two tigers were walking down Sauchiehall Street, and one tiger turned to the other and said, 'I thought you told me this place would be busy?' In the case of the vanishing congregation, once the lion was gone, they all came back in and went on exactly as before. The lion, the uprising of something new, will not be wanted in many churches that have a reputation of being alive. But then I saw this lion going into a church where it was welcomed, and in that church it began to gain strength.

And I saw that the soul of Scotland is going to be strengthened through four things. (This is what I have been shown about what God wants to do in the lives of His people; there are doubtless other parts of the picture.)

Let me tell you what the four things are. First of all, simple **love and affection**. I saw people coming up to this lion and stroking its mane, making a place for it and sitting it down beside them, and as the lion received this affection and love and warmth, it began to be strengthened. You know, the original Struthers of Greenock – the Rev. J. P. Struthers – commented that Christianity would be a lot better off if Christians did 'bonny' things. That's quite good. Church can be a loveless place. The American preacher and teacher Jack Deere speaks of people in churches up and down the land suffering from sheep-bite; one of the first revelations that he received as a pastor was that sheep bite. That's why pastors are given staffs: to beat the sheep over the head, because they bite! Maybe some of you are suffering from sheep-bite; maybe you've bitten other sheep. Maybe you've bitten the shepherd. But the soul of Scotland will be strengthened through simple affection and love between the people of God.

I was visiting not long ago, and speaking to the man and wife of the house when, unnoticed by me, the teenager came through the room. On her way past me she reached down and tickled my tummy. Then she went into the kitchen, and five minutes later she was back giving me a cake that she had made at home economics. It had been a lousy day for me, partly because in the morning I had been at a gathering of ministers (!) marked by so much competitiveness and one-upmanship that I felt dreadful – actually, that's not true: I came away thinking, 'I'm not going back there,' and that made me feel wonderful! But after the heaviness of the morning meeting, what that girl did by tickling my tummy and giving me a cake did me an awful lot more good spiritually than anything that had happened in the morning. I remember Mr Black once saying, 'As I get older, I appreciate folk around me that are kind.' The soul of Scotland will be strengthened by affection and love.

And then I saw that the soul of Scotland will be strengthened by a simple reading, receiving and believing of the **word of God**. I get the impression in many churches that have a name for being renewed in the Spirit that sometimes there's pretty scant regard for this. I remember seeing a video of a Renewal meeting where somebody stood up and said, 'I've got this prophecy from the Lord,' and everybody was agog, waiting for the prophecy. Then somebody else got up and said, 'I just want to read a Bible passage,' and the camera went round the gathering to reveal folk busy with chewing-gum and speaking to each other: they weren't interested in the Bible reading. The word of God has been part of our history, and the soul of Scotland will be strengthened as we come back to this.

Sometimes I've fallen into the trap of not giving the word of God the regard it should have. Not long ago I went through a difficult time. One night when things were at their worst, I was feeling a bit sorry for myself. I was lying in bed trying to think of something to say for the early morning prayer meeting, asking God and praying about it, and nothing was coming. Then I turned on the radio to UCB, and Derek Prince came on. Within two or three minutes his message totally got me up out of the way I was feeling.

How? Simply because he read the word of God, in the last chapter of 2 Timothy, where Paul says, 'Everybody has left me; only Luke is with me.' I thought of myself that day, when dreadful things had been said in the newspaper – and yet throughout the whole day folk had been arriving at the manse delivering chocolates and even red roses. Here was Paul, deserted apart from Luke. And I had been getting fellowship all day!

And then Paul said to Timothy, 'Remember and bring my cloak.' He was cold, and I was lying there under a warm blanket in a centrally heated manse.

He said, 'And remember and bring the parchments and the scrolls with you when you come.' Even at that stage, facing imprisonment, facing imminent death, he was wanting to write encouragement to the rest of the church. And there was I feeling sorry for myself!

Two or three minutes of the word of God lifted me.

I wonder what your relationship with the word of God is like?

The third thing I saw was that the lion felt at home where it could smell its own scent. The scent of the soul of Scotland is the **fear of the Lord**. That was once part of our nation, and it's gone now. And sometimes, again, looking at what passes for Renewal I don't see much of the fear of the Lord. One of the things I've always respected and loved about Struthers is that when I come here I feel the fear of the Lord. I think that there are many churches up and down the land, maybe even including my own, where I could come to a meeting with sin in my life and go home quite happy: but I can't do that here, because you as a people fear the Lord. Where He is feared, He comes. And I feel His presence here.

What is the fear of the Lord? According to Proverbs, it is to hate evil: as simple as that. The soul of Scotland will be strengthened through rediscovering the fear of the Lord. I believe that God said to me on one occasion, 'The days of Ananias and Sapphira are coming back.' Now that's fearful. I think it's what He said, though. And then He said to me this: 'There is always some fool who ignores the warning.' Some of us talk about being 'slain' in the Spirit – Ananias and Sapphira were truly slain. The rest of us by the grace of God have just 'rested'. They were slain, and the church knew the fear of the Lord.

Then lastly I saw a lovely picture as this lion sat amongst the people of God: its face started to beam and grow strong and young again through **worship**. The first few times I came to Struthers, I totally ignored the worship, thinking, 'I'll wait till the sermon – that's what I'm really here for.' But do you know what I found? If I didn't get into God at moment one then I didn't get into Him at all. In my church tradition worship is the sort of thing that you get cleared out of the way along with the intimations. Worship is really coming to hear me, the minister, preach. Something has got to change with that.

I remember being asked to preach at a caravan site once. Though on holiday, I was glad to preach and felt God gave me something to say. I went up to the service, and the worship went on for half an hour ... an hour ... an hour and a half. The longer it went on the more angry I got, thinking, 'I've got something to say, and this is a bit rude!'

And then I felt that God interrupted that train of thought, and He simply said, 'Excuse Me, do you mind if I get the attention tonight?'

'No, Lord.'

And I found that I could say what I wanted to say in half the time and twice as clearly, and He got the glory.

When I talk about worship, I don't just mean the form. I mean intimacy. That's what this lion seemed to be experiencing: intimacy with God. So often we sing about God. But I think one of the marks of what God has been doing lately is that the church is beginning to learn to sing to Him: 'I love You, Lord, and I lift my voice to worship you', intimacy in worship reflecting an intimacy with God Himself. That's what I treasure most, I think, about this place, and whereas once I almost ignored the worship it began to be one of the most precious things on earth to me, to come and get into that from moment one, to sing songs such as you sang twenty years ago, like 'There is a Rose', or 'Sweet Will of God, still fold me closer'.[2] That did something to me. I was refreshed through worship, and I think the soul of Scotland will be refreshed the same way.

The lion is on its feet, something is stirring: but it's still weak. And the soul of Scotland will be strengthened through simple affection and love, through a simple return to the word of God, through rediscovering its own scent, the fear of the Lord, and through an intimacy in worship.

Many of us are longing for more than what we have, even though it is pretty good. From time to time I remember a phrase of C.S. Lewis, 'drippings of grace', which he said are like the scent of a flower that you've not yet found, or the echo of a tune that you've not yet heard, or news from a country that you've not yet visited. I feel that visions are like that. I hope that for you what I've shared tonight will be like the drippings of grace, just to remind you that that flower you've maybe touched at points, that tune that you've maybe heard distantly at times, that country that you've maybe heard news from now and then, is real: it's there. A day of God's power is coming, but we need to strengthen ourselves in God.

In February 1998 I had the privilege of preaching for Kenny over a weekend. I and the group who were with me saw at first hand the evidence of God's moving in Thurso and experienced the power and glory of it as we ministered for various purposes – evangelism, baptism in the Spirit, healing and deliverance.

In the account he gave above, Kenny alluded to a time of difficulty through which he had passed. In fact, after a time of real blessing, there had come a period of very serious persecution. It was as though the devil was enraged, and the attack came from various quarters. There was evidence of occult opposition, and totally unfounded charges of events within the church were splashed in the Press. There were threats of physical violence on two or three occasions. God, however, brought him through, and the power of the opposition was broken.

I have been personally involved in the work of God for over 50 years and have not encountered a situation in conflict with hell as serious in some aspects as that which Kenny faced. The words of Paul very definitely applied:

> *For we wrestle not against flesh and blood, but against principalities, against powers, against the rulers of the darkness of this world, against spiritual wickedness in high places.*   (Ephesians 6:12)

In viewing the successful work that is now in evidence, and the degree to which Kenny is used far beyond Thurso, this critical period should not be overlooked.

Visions of the North

Finally, Kenny was asked to share another vision about which I knew from my friend's letter.

> As I say, I really don't get many visions, but this one, I felt, was significant. It was less than a year-and-a-half ago, but more than a month ago – so I can't quite date it. I felt I was given a vision of the north of Scotland and out towards the sea. I saw rank upon rank upon rank of angels, all in battle array, waiting, ready to move at God's command. But in the front rank there were spaces, and the spaces were for you and me. The angels are ready: they are swift to do their Master's bidding. But it's for us, the sons and daughters of God, to arise and take our place.
>
> And, linked with that, one last vision. I saw a great wave building up to the north of Scotland, a golden wave of the glory of God. It was getting higher and

higher and higher with the prayers of God's people, but it wasn't moving forward one inch.

I started to pray about that and say, 'Well, why, Lord? Why is this wave not moving forward? I see it's getting bigger, that you plan to do something bigger than any of us have yet realized. But why is it not moving forward one inch?'

And then in the vision I saw the sons and daughters of God, Christians that I know, beginning to swim up the wave, and when they got on to the crest of the wave they linked arms and started to do a sort of Christian version of the river dance. As they linked arms in unity and danced like that on the top of the wave, you can guess what happened: the wave began to roll. And it rolled relentlessly. It rolled unstoppably towards the land. And again, linking it with the vision of the angelic army with spaces for us in the front rank, God seemed to say, 'I'm waiting for My sons and daughters to arise in My holiness, in My righteousness.'

In the original vision of the stone lion with Jesus sitting beside it, it was as though He was waiting for us to arise. Although revival is totally sovereign, He is interested in a relationship with His people, and He's looking for us to take our place in the front ranks. He is looking for us to take our place on the crest of the wave, to shine with His righteousness, to shine with His holiness. And then the purpose of God will move with a relentlessness that all of hell won't be able to stop.

For many readers these visions may well strike a familiar chord. It is now around three-and-a-half decades since the American minister Jean Darnall received the series of visions in which she saw pinpricks becoming rivers of fire from the top of Scotland to Land's End, ultimately flowing out to the Continent.[3] Her vision was clear and concrete, and signs of its imminent fulfilment have been multiplying. For example, she envisaged early morning prayer meetings, particularly involving men. It is significant that there had come a point in October 1997 when Kenny felt led to start an early morning prayer meeting from six till seven o'clock each morning. Some very direct and wonderful answers to prayer resulted from this. Stimulated by the South Korean pastor Joshua Paul, many other churches in Scotland also became involved in early morning prayer meetings.

I believe that God has given true revelation to His servant in Thurso. My spirit goes with the things that Kenny has told us. May we be prepared to pay the price that God asks, and be willing, indeed determined, to fill the place that is for us in the front ranks.

Notes

1. From the *Daily Mail*, Friday 2 May 1997. The article cited a survey, 'Beyond Barriers to Belief', co-ordinated by the Rev. Peter Neilson for the General Assembly of the Church of Scotland that year.

2. These songs are still sung in our midst. The old and the new both find a place in our worship. This is not just to accommodate a generation gap! Each type has its own peculiar value.

3. Jean Darnall's vision was first told in her autobiography *Heaven, Here I Come* (Lakeland, 1974) and subsequently with accompanying detail in my own book *Revival: Including the Prophetic Vision of Jean Darnall* (New Dawn Books, 1993).

Appendix on Phobias

Readers may be interested to know how deliverance from phobia works. A phobia is a type of fear, and it is amazing the number of people who are affected by fear of one kind or another. There is a natural fear which has nothing to do with phobias. The phobic type itself can be very general, or it can be particular. Often when a phobia grips a person it is related to a particular incident, such as some kind of traumatic experience. When that happens, there is a psychological defence mechanism that comes into operation. The fear is pressed down into the subconscious, where instead of it dying it lingers and 'suppurates'. We defend ourselves by building a kind of barrier against it, but in fact we don't get rid of it that way, and frequently the trouble erupts in the dream world at night, or at times when we're not prepared: it just suddenly comes to the surface and grips and binds. When God deals with a phobia, instead of being pushed down it comes right up and goes right out.

Much of what I have learned of this subject has not come through books but rather from experience and, I believe, from revelation. My normal method is to ask the sufferer to picture the past and relive it. In ministering to individuals I ask them to go back to the time when the phobia first affected them. I ask them to face their difficulty at its worst point. This can be unnerving, but I assure them that they will only have to face it for a moment or two, and then it can be gone for ever. Again and again I have seen this happen.

It is important that fear is uncovered at its deepest level. If it is only skimmed at the surface it will recur. As the person looks at the enemy face to face, the spiritual ministry comes into operation. Up to that point much is quite simply technical, and is similar to, though probably more direct than, the technique used in the medical profession; there is nothing particularly spiritual in the instruction up to that point. But the spiritual, the miraculous, side comes in at this point. This next part cannot be done artificially. I frequently become conscious of the near coming of Christ, and I say to the sufferer, 'Now Christ has come, and instead of your standing alone facing your fear, He is here, and the phobia and Christ cannot stay together. Either it will go, and you will be left free, or He will not stay with it. Make your choice – Christ or the phobia!' Again and again I find that Christ stands with the person. He goes back, as it were, into the past where the thing has happened, and I can actually feel the phobia depart; it usually goes out in a very few moments. Normally two minutes is enough, and the healing is complete, with no recurrence of the problem; but I do advise people, if they should ever feel apprehensive of its return, to put Christ between them and the phobia, and they will be perfectly safe. I should point out that people with phobias usually mistakenly think that they fear snakes or spiders or heights or flying or whatever, when in reality they suffer from the fear of the fear. It is from this horror that God sets free.

Over the years I have found that great numbers of people have been liberated. Again and again I tell audiences of hundreds that I want them to see a demonstration of the power of God right on the spot. I assure them that if they come for ministry, an average of about 98 per cent will be set free. It is amazing to see the effect. In a comparatively new company many will respond. In our own companies very few now do, because there are very few people left with phobias. In new situations, after hearing one or two testimonies, it's amazing to see just how keen people are to be healed. As they come, they are allowed when they are set free to tell the company what has happened, and of course that encourages others in the audience. The healings take place immediately and the glory of God comes with the functioning of the ministry.

There are times when people who may be in the line for ministry drop out, and on enquiry we find the phobia has in fact left them. The phobia has, of course, a demon connection. The demon senses, I suppose, the near coming of Christ, and is terrified, and sometimes flees even before there is actual ministry. Deliverance from phobias is one of the easiest forms of deliverance in which I have been involved. There are cases of deep demon possession which sometimes can cause a great deal of difficulty, but phobias normally go very, very easily indeed.

Note to Readers

If you would like to enquire further about issues raised in this book or if you feel that the compiler could be of help, you are invited to write to him at: 27 Denholm Street, Greenock, PA16 8RH, Scotland, or telephone 01475-729668 or 01475-7874342.

It may also be of interest to know that Hugh Black is normally involved in five conferences in Scotland each year – New Year, Easter, July, August and October. Friends gather from many parts of Britain. An open invitation is extended to all and particularly to those interested in the baptism in the Holy Spirit and related themes. Details will be provided on enquiry (tel. 0141-339-3543).

Other Books by Hugh Black

The Baptism in the Spirit and Its Effects   £4.99

Used in bringing people into the baptism in the Spirit and described as one of the clearest, most incisive books on the subject. This expanded edition includes evidence that Finney, Moody and Spurgeon spoke in tongues, and narrates miraculous effects of the baptism in the lives of Jimmy Lunan and Allan Wiggins.

Reflections on the Gifts of the Spirit   £2.75

Deals in an original way with its subject. The chapters on miracles, healings and discernment (with exorcism) have roused great interest and led to positive action. Anecdotes and illustrations have been much appreciated.

Reflections on a Song of Love   £1.25

A highly original commentary on 1 Corinthians 13. The drawing power of love pervades this fascinating study. The author shows very clearly how this chapter fully supports and in no way detracts from the doctrine of Pentecost.

A Trumpet Call to Women   **£2.50**

Presents a strong case from Scripture for greater involvement of women in ministry. It throws much light on those portions which on the surface seem to put women in a subject role. It includes the testimony of Elizabeth H. Taylor, a lady much used of God. A stirring book, demanding a response – a call to action.

Consider Him   **£2.25**

Considers a number of the qualities of Christ. He Himself seems to speak from the pages of the book, both in the main text and in the testimony of Jennifer Jack, whose selfless presentation truly leaves the reader to consider Christ.

Battle for the Body   **£2.95**

It will take courage to face the truths highlighted in this original approach to fundamental issues of sanctification. The second part presents the powerful testimony of John Hamilton – a preacher widely known and loved.

The Clash of Tongues: With Glimpses of Revival   **£2.75**

Part One is a commentary on 1 Corinthians 14. It deals in detail with some of the more difficult questions. Part Two deals with the relationship between revival and Pentecost and refers to the 1939 and 1949 revivals in Lewis, introducing a number of people who were involved in the first of these – particularly Mary MacLean, whose remarkable testimony is related. This book may particularly appeal to people studiously inclined.

The Incomparable Christ   **£2.75**

Part One deals with the gospel. It faces honestly the questions of Christ's resurrection and that of all men.

It deals in a direct way with the doctrine of hell and eternal judgment, and gives practical instruction on the way of salvation. Part Two presents the remarkable testimonies of two young ladies.

Gospel Vignettes £2.95

Focuses attention on various facets of the gospel, with chapter titles like: Ye Must Be Born Again, The Life-Giving Water, Weighed in the Balances, Behold I Stand at the Door and Knock, The Hour of Decision. Includes testimonies of three people whose lives have been transformed by Christ, to one of whom Christ Himself appeared. Useful in the gospel, but introducing the pentecostal dimension.

Reflections from Abraham £2.50

Outlines spiritual principles seen in the life of Abraham. It deals with his call and ours, the mountain as distinct from the valley life, intercession, Lot in Sodom, the sacrifice of Isaac and the way of faith. Part Two tells of the action of God in the life of Dorothy Jennings, to whom Abraham has been of particular significance.

Reflections from Moses: With the Testimony of Dan McVicar £2.99

Part One shows the outworking of spiritual principles such as the calling and training of a man of God, the need to start from holy ground, deliverance from bondage, and the consequences of Moses' failure in a critical hour. Part Two presents the well-known evangelist Dan McVicar's story in his own words. The conversion of this militant communist and the intervention of God in the lives of his parents make thrilling reading.

Christ the Deliverer   £2.99

Deals with both physical and spiritual deliverance. It includes a number of remarkable testimonies to healing, e.g. from blindness, manic depression, ME, rheumatoid arthritis, spinal injury, phobias, nightmares. It speaks of the appearance of angels, touches on revival and analyses the theory of 'visualization'.

Christian Fundamentals   £3.50

Part One deals with the individual and his needs in the realms of salvation, baptism in the Spirit, and deliverance. Testimonies include that of the author's daughter Mary Black. Part Two focuses on the outflow of the life of God to meet the needs of others through vocal, hidden and open power ministries. The end times are the subject of Part Three.

Reflections from David   £3.75

This searching book shows a man after God's own heart in the glory of his achievements and the tragedy of his failings. Divine retribution and forgiveness, the joy of deliverance, and the action of God in present-day lives are all examined.

Pioneers of the Spiritual Way   £4.99

From a lost Eden our race walked a lost road, occasionally experiencing higher things as pioneers of the spiritual way led upwards. The impassable barrier between God and man was finally removed as the last Adam blasted a way through: Christ, bringing many sons to glory.

Revival:
Including the Prophetic Vision of Jean Darnall   £3.99

Some of the great revivals of the past are reviewed with their enduring principles and changing patterns. Revival comes nearer as we are confronted with more recent movements of God. The celebrated vision of Jean Darnall has left many with a feeling of keen expectation for coming days.

Revival: Personal Encounters £4.50

From the treasure chest of memory the author brings a series of revival-related incidents. We hear of Studd, Burton and Salter and of revival in the Congo and Rwanda. More is revealed of the moving of God in Lewis and at an unusual Scottish school camp. A contemporary scene in Brazil brings revival very close. The highly original testimony of Alison Speirs brings the fact and challenge right to our doorstep.

Revival: Living in the Realities £3.99

For a revived or a revival-conscious people a high level of Christian living is immediately presented. The experience of revival has to be outworked. This book ponders issues such as spiritual warfare, what it means to be imitators of Christ, the need to progress from forgiveness to love for those who do us harm, and the mystery of the love of God itself. An unusual and thought-provoking book.

E.H. Taylor, A Modern Christian Mystic:
Sayings and Recollections (ed. by Hugh Black) £4.50

A sequel to *Trumpet Call to Women*, this highly unusual book contains insights into a wide range of spiritual themes on the part of one who was much used in predictive prophecy and in leading people into the baptism in the Spirit and deliverance, and especially into a deep knowledge of Christ.

War in Heaven and Earth £6.99

This book illuminates the subject of spiritual warfare both at the 'ground level' of day-to-day living where the devil's weapons are met with the weapons of Christ, and at the unseen level of conflict where the power of Christ breaks the hold of spiritual entities over specific territorial areas.

A View from the Floor   **£5.99**

What happens when the power of the Holy Spirit comes upon someone? The first of a series, this book of testimonies traces the effects of a spiritual movement which began in November 1994 and continues to the present time. It is fascinating to learn some of the detail of what happens when we find ourselves on God's operating table.

Further Views from the Floor
(co-author: Dr A.H. Black)   **£5.99**

Weeping, laughing, singing, dancing ... whatever is happening in the Church? This book attempts through many personal testimonies to probe beneath the surface of the external manifestations. It strikingly portrays the reality of a Christ-centred revelation of God to lives in need or simply desiring to know more of Him.

Book Orders

New Dawn Bookshop, 10A Jamaica Street, Greenock
Renfrewshire, PA15 1YB, Scotland
Telephone 01475 729668   *Fax* 01475 728145
Website www.struthers-church.org
Email bookshop@struthers-church.org

ORDER FORM

Please send me books by Hugh B. Black indicated below:

Quantity	Title	Price
_____	The Baptism in the Spirit and Its Effects	£4.99
_____	Reflections on the Gifts of the Spirit	£2.75
_____	Reflections on a Song of Love (a commentary on 1 Corinthians 13)	£1.25
_____	A Trumpet Call to Women	£2.50
_____	Consider Him (Twelve Qualities of Christ)	£2.25
_____	Battle for the Body	£2.95
_____	The Clash of Tongues: With Glimpses of Revival	£2.75
_____	The Incomparable Christ	£2.75
_____	Gospel Vignettes	£2.95
_____	Reflections from Abraham	£2.50
_____	Reflections from Moses: With the Testimony of Dan McVicar	£2.99
_____	Christ the Deliverer	£2.99

(*cont. overleaf*)

_____	Christian Fundamentals	£3.50
_____	Reflections from David	£3.75
_____	Pioneers of the Spiritual Way	£4.99
_____	Revival: Including the Prophetic Vision of Jean Darnall	£3.99
_____	Revival: Personal Encounters	£4.50
_____	Revival: Living in the Realities	£3.99
_____	E.H. Taylor: A Modern Christian Mystic	£4.50
_____	War in Heaven and Earth	£6.99
_____	A View from the Floor	£5.99
_____	Further Views from the Floor	£5.99
_____	Evidence from the Floor: with prophetic insights of Kenny Borthwick	£6.99

Name . . . .

Address . . . .

. . . .

. . . . Post Code . . . .

UK orders:
Please enclose payment including 60p p & p for one book plus 30p for each additional book.

Overseas orders:
Please pay on receipt (including postage at cost).